THEIR ROYAL HIGHNESSES

ANTHONY HOLDEN

Their Royal Highnesses

THE PRINCE & PRINCESS OF WALES

WEIDENFELD AND NICOLSON

London

Printed and bound by Butler & Tanner Ltd
Frome and London

For my parents

CONTENTS

ILLUSTRATIONS

Cecil Beaton takes the first portrait (*BBC Hulton Picture Library*).

The Royal Family enjoys a Balmoral summer (*The Times*).

A happy, relaxed interlude with the Mountbattens in Malta (*Syndication International*).

Just another undergraduate in the Trinity College freshmen's photo (*Serge Lemoine*).

Leaders of fashion?: the last Prince of Wales, the future King Edward VIII and Duke of Windsor, in a snappy jersey (*Press Association*).

His successor in a safer grey suit (*Peter Grugeon, Camera Press*).

A comparative study in toppers: the future King Edward VIII (*Press Association*) and Prince Charles (*Tim Graham*).

The Prince of Wales meets Farrah Fawcett (*Press Association*).

With Lady Jane Wellesley (*Syndication International*) ...

... and with Lady Sarah Spencer, sister of the bride (*Syndication International*).

On duty in India (*Tim Graham*).

Off duty at Sandringham (*Syndication International*) and at Klosters (*Syndication International*).

Lady Diana Spencer (*Sun*).

Diana leaving her flat at Coleherne Court (*Keystone*).

Pursuit by paparazzi (*Keystone*).

Fleeing ... but where? Diana climbs into her famous Mini Metro (*Syndication International*) ...

... then stalls it (*Press Association*).

Charles hunts in Cheshire (*Tim Graham*).

Diana strolls round her family's estate at Althorp (*Tim Graham*).

Charles and Diana leave Lambourn after their dawn rendezvous (*three photos by Tim Graham*).

Diana's father and stepmother join the crowd outside Buckingham Palace after the engagement announcement (*Rex Features*).

The happy couple about to dine with their grandmothers (*Syndication International*).

Inspector Paul Officer keeps a watchful eye on his master's bride-to-be (*Tim Graham*).

In the paddock at Sandown (*Serge Lemoine*).

Diana makes her first appearance with other royals (*Tim Graham*).

Disaster at Sandown: Prince Charles takes a tumble (*Rex Features*) ...

... and hangs his head in shame (*Tim Graham*).

The dress that stunned the world (*Rex Features*).

Diana meets Princess Grace of Monaco (*Tim Graham*).

ILLUSTRATIONS

ACKNOWLEDGMENTS

This book is intended to be a companion volume to my biography of Prince Charles, *Charles, Prince of Wales* (1979), to which I humbly refer readers anxious for more detail of Prince Charles's life so far than they find in Chapter Three herewith. The two books inevitably overlap in occasional places, but the only item reprinted directly from the earlier work is the present Appendix A on Prince Charles's descent (formerly Appendix C). For this, and for his help with Appendix B (Lady Diana Spencer's descent), I again thank the fount of all wisdom on matters genealogical, Sir Iain Moncreiffe of that Ilk.

Much of the information for the present volume comes from those who helped me with the first one, for which I conducted more than two hundred interviews over a period of two years. My thanks should therefore be repeated to all those in the hefty acknowledgments list of *Charles, Prince of Wales* – and renewed, with feeling, to those of them, and others around the Royal Family, who have since kept in touch. They would not thank me for naming them here.

My gratitude, also, to the many readers who have written to me with helpful suggestions, many of which have been built into the present volume. I must especially thank Sir Anthony Gray, secretary of the Duchy of Cornwall, for a voluminous and highly enjoyable transatlantic correspondence which cleared up a few misunderstandings.

I am again deeply grateful to many people at Weidenfeld and Nicolson, primarily to Lord Weidenfeld himself, for his encouragement and hospitality; to John Curtis, for initiating this book, and seeing me through the dark days of Prince Charles's indecision; to Linda Osband, whose editing has improved it beyond recognition; to Rosalind Lewis and Camilla Horne for bludgeoning people into taking an interest in it; and to many other friends I have made in Weidenfeld's London office and around the national sales team. On the publishers' behalf, as well as my own, I must thank Messrs Wedgwood of Stoke-on-Trent for their generous assistance with both volumes.

I am again deeply grateful to Hilary Rubinstein of A.P. Watt Ltd and Perry

ACKNOWLEDGMENTS

Knowlton of Curtis Brown (New York), for their professional advice and personal friendship; to the editors of the *Observer* and *The Times*, Donald Trelford, and Harold Evans, for tolerating my curious fascination with princes as well as presidents; and to my wife Amanda, without whose long-suffering tolerance I'd never get anything done. The present volume would not have been possible without the painstaking work of my research assistant, Ann Wilson, nor would it look so nice without the skilful picture research of Lynda Poley.

For especial help with the present book – in some cases, for helping me make time to write it – I would like to thank: Helen Friedmann, Joseph Friedmann, Andrea Hellard, Peter Pringle, Eleanor Randolph, David Blundy, Anne Marris and Simon Barber. For their generous assistance, despite the fact that I was again making a temporary incursion into their jealously-guarded territory, I am particularly grateful to Britain's two leading 'Charles-watchers', James Whitaker of the *Star* and Harry Arnold of the *Sun*. I must also thank Messrs William Rees-Mogg, Rupert Murdoch and Harold Evans for their leads as I gumshoed my way towards The Great Fleet Street Whodunnit (pp. 65–66).

Finally, I must again acknowledge the courtesy of the Buckingham Palace press office, especially Her Majesty The Queen's press secretary, Michael Shea, and assistant press secretary, Warwick Hutchings. Mr Shea tells me that everything I write on the subject of Prince Charles has caused him enormous trouble, 'as everyone seems to believe it's true'. Taking the remark as a compliment, I must apologize to him for that imposition – and also to His Royal Highness The Prince of Wales, whose response to the reappearance of my shadow in his footsteps has been characteristically civil (most recently in Australia in April). I hereby promise them both to disappear from their lives forthwith, forever. And I would like, by way of a fond farewell, to wish the Prince and Princess of Wales every happiness.

Their loyal servant,
ANTHONY HOLDEN

'A princely marriage is the brilliant edition
of a universal fact, and as such it rivets mankind'

– Walter Bagehot, *The English Constitution*

PROLOGUE

'Harris, I am not well, pray get me a glass of brandy,' said the Prince of Wales on first meeting his bride-to-be, the evening before their wedding, in April 1795. The sight of Princess Caroline of Brunswick-Wolfenbuttel had proved quite a shock, and she was to plague the future King George IV for the rest of their married life. But times, and the monarchy, have changed. Nearly two centuries later, Prince Charles's future subjects are about to witness the first 'unarranged' marriage of a Prince of Wales in history.

At a meeting of the Privy Council on 27 March 1981 Queen Elizabeth II gave her formal assent, as was her obligation under the Royal Marriages Act of 1772, to the wedding of her son Charles, Prince of Wales, to the Lady Diana Spencer. The issue of the Royal Warrant, under the Great Seal of England, inched forward the momentous preparations for the allotted day, four months later. Already it was being billed as 'the last great state occasion of the century'. In pomp and circumstance, said the protocol experts, it would outshine even Elizabeth's Coronation in 1953. The principality of Wales, for the first time in more than seventy years, would again have a Princess. Since 24 February, when the engagement was officially announced, Britain and the Commonwealth have been making ready a right royal welcome for Diana, their future Queen.

The last Princess of Wales, later George V's Queen Mary, never made a speech or used a telephone in her life. Less than thirty years after her death, the new Princess will be the first future Queen of England to have once worked for a living. Among her children will be the first future monarch ever to have been descended from all the British Kings and Queens who had issue: for Diana brings Stuart blood to the royal line, the only royal blood it lacks, as well as links on the family tree with Charlemagne and Bonnie Prince Charlie, Humphrey Bogart and Rudolf Valentino. Her father, the eighth Earl Spencer, felt moved to call Diana 'a superb physical specimen'. That, saving her grace, she surely is. She is also the very model of a modern Princess.

The last time London saw the wedding of a Prince of Wales, in the spring of

[17]

1863, Alfred, Lord Tennyson was foremost among those who got quite carried away by it all:

> Sea-kings' daughter from over the sea, Alexandra!
> Saxon and Norman and Dane are we,
> But all of us Danes in our welcome of thee, Alexandra!
> ... Sea-kings' daughter, as happy as fair,
> Blissful bride of a blissful heir,
> Oh joy to the people, and joy to the throne,
> Come to us, love us, and make us your own!

Etcetera, etcetera. *The Times* did not quite share His Lordship's enthusiasm. The royal carriages, wrote its court correspondent, 'looked old and shabby, and the horses very poor, with no trappings, not even rosettes, and no outriders. In short, the shabbiness of the whole cortège was beyond anything one could imagine, everybody asking: Who is the Master of the Horse?' He denounced 'that singularly ill-appointed establishment known as the Royal Mews', and declared that 'the servants, carriages and cattle selected to convey the Danish Princess through joyful London came from its very dregs.'

There is no danger of that on 29 July 1981, when London and the country will be lavishly *en fête* for the first wedding of an heir to the throne to an English rose for three hundred years. As has so often been true of recent royal weddings, particularly that of the Prince's parents in 1947, the celebrations will take place at a time of national austerity. This time round *The Times*, after the Thatcher Government's March Budget, struck a cautious, more contemporary note:

> The royal marriage in July will be a happy, cheerful and cheering event. Pageantry and making merry are of its essence and part of its almost assured popularity. No one wants austerity for that wedding day. But the stage management and the ballyhoo of press and television coverage call for discretion. A much larger part of the people than usual will be going through hard times. They could easily be made to feel excluded from what should be a national occasion. A public holiday is no treat for the out-of-work. A celebration surrounding the future King and his bride that somehow comes across as an extravaganza for the grand, the rich and gilded youth would leave a sour taste in many mouths.

There were similar words of warning in 1947, when the Treasury even tried to talk Buckingham Palace – unsuccessfully – into 'an austerity wedding'. But as the big day approached, the mystic spell of royalty worked its magic, and the ranks of the doubters thinned out. On 20 November 1947, Britain was glued to its wireless sets; next day, newspapers sold out at dawn. The indifferent, even the cynical had been seen – despite themselves – purchasing royal tea trays and dabbing moist eyes. And so it will be in 1981.

Not for many, by 29 July, the sentiments of the *Morning Star*, the Communist daily newspaper, on 25 February: 'Lady Diana Spencer is to sacrifice her independence to a domineering layabout for the sake of a few lousy foreign holidays.' Nor will Labour councillors endear themselves to their electors by voting to 'boycott the occasion' – though quite how you do that is unclear – as did some in Yorkshire after the engagement was announced. Even the fortune-tellers, normally the most sycophantic of royal commentators, saw clouds in their crystal balls. 'Lady's Di's face spells trouble for Charles' cautioned 're-nowned face-reader' Sherry Lane in the *News of the World*; 'Svetlana' of the *Washington Post* waxed even more doom-laden: 'No court astrologer would have ever advised them to be married in July, since Prince Charles *and* Lady Diana have strong Uranus transits on their charts. In addition, the last week in July is sandwiched between two eclipses, and those are not good auspices under which to enter any permanent relationship.' Much more in the spirit of things was the suggestion of Mr George Foulkes, MP for South Ayrshire, who urged that Lady Diana should support British industry on her wedding day by wearing jeans up the aisle of St Paul's; removing his tongue from his cheek, Mr Foulkes later conceded that there were four denim-making factories in his constituency.

More than five hundred million people around the world will be watching Lady Diana as she promises to love, honour and obey Charles, Prince of Wales, Earl of Chester, Duke of Cornwall, Duke of Rothesay, Earl of Carrick, Baron Renfrew, Lord of the Isles and Great Steward of Scotland, Knight of the Most Noble Order of the Garter, Knight of the Most Ancient and Most Noble Order of the Thistle, Great Master and Principal Knight Grand Cross of the Most Honourable Order of the Bath. And they will be wishing her – as the people of Wales wished Alexandra, on presenting her with a leek-shaped bracelet one hundred and eighteen years ago: '*Duw Cadwo Ein Tywosogos*' – 'God Keep Our Princess'.

CHAPTER ONE

The King and Di

'EVEN I don't know what's going on,' said Queen Elizabeth II rather testily, when asked by intimates about her son and heir's latest romance. It was the autumn of 1980, and the Prince of Wales himself had disappeared to India on an oft-postponed and long-awaited tour. Behind him, in Buckingham Palace as in the popular press, he left fevered speculation about his friendship with nineteen-year-old Diana Spencer, the latest in a long line of candidates for his future Queen.

Across the world, in the foot-hills of the Himalayas, Charles had slipped away from his hosts, his public and his press for a few days' mountain-trekking in as much isolation as is ever possible for the heir to the British throne. It had been a gruelling tour so far, with several protest demonstrations, a few political incidents, and even some deaths among the uncontrollable crowds fighting for a glimpse of him. To those who knew him well, he had seemed unusually on edge.

When he came back down from the mountains, however, the rest of the royal party noticed a marked change in the Prince, a sudden calm and confidence which seemed to go beyond the mere rigours of a turbulent royal tour. 'It was as if', said one, 'some huge burden had suddenly been lifted from his shoulders.' It was as if, agreed others in retrospect, he had been wrestling with some major decision, and had at last resolved it. And so he had.

Charles said nothing to anyone, including his closest advisers, and was not even ready yet to share his thoughts with his parents. When he arrived back at the Palace, late at night, he was told the Queen was anxious to see him early the next morning. There could be only one thing she wanted to see him about. He got up just a few hours later, at dawn, despite his jet lag, and drove down to Highgrove, his country house in Gloucestershire, to spend the day with the local hunt. His mother, when she awoke to the news, was not best pleased.

Ten days later, the Royal Family foregathered as usual for its annual Christmas house party at Windsor. Of all their several and seasonal homes, Windsor is the one least vulnerable to the prying eyes and ears of the press. To the Queen, who spent the wartime years of her childhood there, it is the most private of her residences, the one she most likes to call home. So it was at Windsor, seizing this psychological advantage, that Prince Charles told his parents he was seriously thinking of asking Diana Spencer to marry him. Had he finally made up his mind? No, not quite: he was sure of his own feelings, but not yet totally of hers. He needed a few more quiet moments with her, of the kind so hard to arrange with discretion. Would his mother invite Diana to Sandringham, to join them for New Year? Of course, she said, but this time he must not linger too long over his decision. 'The idea of this romance going on for another year is intolerable for everyone concerned.'

It soon became clear, at Sandringham, what she meant. The world's press was there in force, taking advantage of the public right-of-way which crosses the royal estate, hounding the Royals' every outdoor excursion. What Charles later called 'a military operation' went into action, to spirit Diana in and out of the place without the mob overwhelming her. It was not altogether successful. The Queen, who does not entirely share the popular view that she and her family are public property at all times, grew increasingly angry. For all her proven *savoir-faire* at public relations, she still believed that photographers had no right to pitch camp in her privacy, even on what is legally public property. Stung by a pre-Christmas report that Charles and Diana had enjoyed a secret 'love-tryst' on the royal train, and subsequently by the newspaper's refusal to retract its story, the Queen demanded that Fleet Street's editors call off their dogs. Not this time, ma'am, editorialized the daily papers. We've got a job to do, and we're staying. In a remarkable flash of public temper, unprecedented in her three decades on the throne, Elizabeth II one day rounded angrily on the royal press corps and shouted: 'Oh, I do wish you people would go away.'

Charles himself caught the royal mood, and added what was for him a most uncharacteristic message to the people whose faces he had come to know so well. 'A happy new year to you,' he shouted to those journalists known to themselves as 'Charles-watchers', 'but a particularly nasty one to your editors.' Fleet Street next day waxed indignant, while the Royal Family continued to fume. One reporter claimed that her car had been peppered by royal gunshot. Whatever the rights and wrongs of the episode, it scarcely created an atmosphere conducive to royal romance.

Throughout January, Diana went through the ultimate in testings for membership of the Royal Family. Each day she braved, with dignity and discretion, an ordeal by camera and notebook as she travelled to her job at a Pimlico kindergarten. Despite it all, she and Charles managed several secret meetings – at a house he owns in central London, at Highgrove, and at the Queen Mother's home in Scotland. Diana told Charles she planned to flee for a while to Australia, where her mother has a home, for a much-needed break from all the attention. She had made arrangements to travel on Friday 6 February. Charles, who would be away skiing in the meantime, invited her to dine alone with him at Buckingham Palace, a couple of evenings before she had to leave.

And there the question was finally, as they say, popped. Diana accepted at once, but Charles urged her to 'think the whole thing over' in Australia, lest on mature reflection it prove 'too awful' a prospect. With her mother at her side – the dominant figure in her life, for all the trauma of her parents' divorce – Diana never wavered. Three years before, she had thought she might one day see her elder sister Sarah crowned Charles's Queen. Now it was all offered to her: the tedium, the loneliness, the frustrations, the lack of privacy – all of which Charles had been at pains to point out – as much as the pomp, the privilege, the wealth and the adulation. It was, she decided, what she wanted. 'It is', she corrected herself later, 'what I want.'

On Saturday 21 February, at a secret dinner party at Windsor Castle, Lady Diana was the Queen's guest of honour at a table crammed with contemporary British royalty. Princess Alexandra and her husband, Angus Ogilvy, joined the entire immediate family to toast the royal couple. The announcement, it was decided, should be delayed no longer. Charles had gone through the proper motions of asking the permission of the bride's father, Earl Spencer. Diana herself, she told them, had never had a moment's doubt. After all the months of discretion and dissimulation, she yearned for a public chance to say so.

It came three days later, on 24 February, at 11 am, when the Lord

Chamberlain stepped forward at the beginning of a routine investiture ceremony in Buckingham Palace. The Queen looked on in a rosy glow as Lord Maclean told the audience that Her Majesty had asked him to read to them 'an announcement that is being made at this moment':

> It is with the greatest pleasure that the Queen and the Duke of Edinburgh announce the betrothal of their beloved son, the Prince of Wales, to Lady Diana Spencer, daughter of the Earl Spencer and the Hon. Mrs Shand-Kydd.

The news was not unexpected, but the timing of the announcement caught everyone off guard. Its immediate repercussions went well beyond the happy carnival of chaos in newspaper offices around the world, and the ineluctable gathering of a large throng outside the Palace railings – braving, as so often on these occasions, a freezing cold day, and delighted to be joined by the bride's father making home movies. At 11.05 am, in its offices just a mile from the Palace, the Ulster Weaving Company proudly unveiled to the press its ready-made Charles and Diana tea towels. A record company announced plans for the reissue of Paul Anka's twenty-year-old hit – older, as it happened, than the lady herself – 'Diana'. The bonanza was on.

In the City of London, the Stock Exchange quickly reflected the curious array of beneficiaries of these rare royal bean-feasts. Shares in Royal Worcester China, which would be churning out everything from commemorative mugs to bone china 'Happy Couple' dinner services, jumped 23p to 293. The news, said the long-established Staffordshire pottery firm of Wedgwood, traditional manufacturers of high-class royal icons of all shapes and sizes, came as 'a lifesaver' at a very difficult time. The company had been on a three-day week during this low point of the Thatcher years; now it would be back on full production, with overtime. Wedgwood shares closed up by 5p. It was a good day, too, for Royal Doulton, whose plans included a limited-edition Royal Crown Derby loving cup, to go on sale at £750.

Holdings in hotel companies and the big West End stores also rose in anticipation of the inevitable influx of tourists. It was, said the chairman of the British Tourist Authority, Sir Henry Marking, 'just the fillip' the industry needed. There were smiles in the board room of Birmingham Mint, makers of commemorative coins and medallions, and for the Black and Edgington camping group, producers of marquees and – yes – flags. Perhaps the most popular of the day's beneficiaries by close of business were the breweries, one of whom announced a new brand of real ale in honour of the occasion.

Would Moss Bros, first port of call for those in temporary need of a morning suit, be rubbing their hands with glee? The Stock Market thought so: their shares rose from 180p to 187. Said the chairman, Monty Moss: 'Plenty of our suits will be going to the wedding. The Commonwealth guests usually hire ... they take our biggest sizes.' He expressed relief that the date would be late July: 'Any earlier, and all our suits would have been at Ascot.'

Eyre and Spottiswoode announced plans for publication of two 'special' Bibles – standard version at £6.95, and £9.95 for the 'superior' imitation leather edition with silver trimmings. Liberty's of Regent Street did the right thing and had their tea towel approved by the Palace, although the Lord Chamberlain had temporarily lifted the usual restrictions on the use of royal faces and insignia for commercial gain. Liberty headscarves, silk of course, would be available at £15 each. Skycrafts of Stratford-upon-Avon planned a Charles-and-Di kite – yours for just £2. And Readicut International, a Yorkshire textile firm which had been on hard times, rushed into production thousands of do-it-yourself wall-hanging kits. But their plans for a Charles-and-Di rug fell foul of the Lord Chamberlain's Office: it is not acceptable, they were told, to have people walking on the royal face.

In Portsmouth Harbour, the minesweeper HMS *Bronington* fired a twenty-one-gun salute in honour of its former skipper and his bride. At the Synod of the Church of England, the Archbishop of Canterbury, Dr Robert Runcie, broke into a debate – appropriately enough, on marriage – to pass on the news. One of the regrets of his relatively new role as Archbishop, said Dr Runcie, was that he no longer conducted marriage services; now he had a particularly august one to look forward to.

Back at Buckingham Palace, the congratulatory telegrams began to flood in. Palace staff had, in fact, enjoyed a couple of hours' prior warning of the announcement – not by any privileged early intelligence, but by the discovery in their offices that morning that the fridges had overnight been stocked with champagne. As Charles and Diana met the press in happier circumstances, and strolled on the Palace lawns for photographers, Madame Tussauds lodged their formal application for a measurement session with the bride-to-be. They wanted her at her Prince's side, in wax as in the flesh, in time for the big day.

Across the Atlantic, in Washington, there was some consternation that the new First Lady, Nancy Reagan, appeared to have anticipated the engagement secret. A month before, it was revealed, she had ordered from a British porcelain firm 'customized Charles and Diana roses', to adorn the White House table at a dinner scheduled for the Prince two months later.

In the Commons, the Prime Minister broke the news to scenes of suitably loyal acclamation, repeated with even more fervour in the House of Lords. The lone dissenting voice, not for the first or the last time, was that of the crusading anti-monarchist MP, Willie Hamilton of Fife, Central, who expressed dismay that 'we're in for six months of mush'. Mr Hamilton made a more telling criticism later in the day, when the latest unemployment figures showed that Britain's jobless had risen to 2.5 million, a figure unprecedented since the Great Depression of the 1930s. Queen and Prime Minister, he charged, had 'connived' at the timing of the royal announcement to distract attention from the Thatcher Government's industrial and economic woes.

'During the next few months we shall have further distractions from the results of the Government's disastrous policies as the celebrations get under way,' said Mr Hamilton. 'There will be no question of cash limits [for the royal wedding], a six per cent restriction, or worry about the impact on the public sector borrowing requirement. The sky will be the limit. And the British people, deferential as always, will wallow in it. The winter of discontent is now being replaced by the winter of phoney romance.'

Clearly, a July wedding for Charles and Diana would indeed give a morale-boost to what otherwise looked like being a long, hot summer for the Thatcher Government. Thirty-two years earlier, in November 1948, the birth of the heir to the throne had brought some welcome cheer to a depressed, rationed post-war Britain – in particular, to a London still recovering from the Blitz. Now, with his wedding, that wheel had turned full circle.

In November 1947, a year before Charles's birth, the wedding of Princess Elizabeth to Prince Philip of Greece and Denmark had similarly enlivened the gloomy post-war scene. It had been the worst winter in living memory, with snow falling solidly from January to March, critical coal shortages, and even such staples as potatoes rationed to 3 lb per adult per week. 'There are the makings here of immense discontent,' warned the *Manchester Guardian*. 'The way to recovery runs on a knife edge. Our democratic system has never been put to a harder test.'

Nevertheless, Buckingham Palace felt bullish enough to turn aside a Treasury proposal for 'an austerity wedding'. Elizabeth had eight bridesmaids in dresses 'spotted with pearls', and mounted police had difficulty keeping the royal procession route clear of people who 'scampered forward laughing and cheering'. Clearly, said the *Guardian* next day, 'somebody showed poor understanding of public opinion in supposing that because most people are shabby and constrained, they would prefer the Princess to have had an austerity wedding.'

'One might have guessed', continued that great liberal newspaper, 'that republicanism had a surer future. But there really does seem to be in most of the human race a profound instinct to single out some few of the species – to differentiate and idealize them, and to make them the object of a loyalty which no process of thought can either justify or destroy.'

Plus ça change. Thirty-three years later, on the announcement of the engagement of the Prince of Wales, the *Daily Telegraph* declared: 'For a nation more than ever starved of symbols of hope and goodness in its public life, the royal example, far from fading, becomes more important.... With so many commoners who hate, it matters more than ever that a Prince who loves should one day sit upon the throne of Britain.' And *The Times*: 'It is something to give pleasure to all but the stoniest of hearts; and it is fitting that the Prince of Wales should enter married life when one considers the extent to which the monarchy is now regarded as an exemplar of the family.' And the *Economist*: 'Send her victorious. Happy and glorious. Long to help to reign over us. God save the next Queen.'

The *Guardian*, thirty-three years on, coyly affected the indifference of its gentrified, middle-class readers: 'A few midsummer trumpets will hardly come amiss.... How is one young and happy couple different from the hundreds of others whose engagement yesterday has gone uncelebrated? It is hard to say, except that some things seem natural and some perverse. Not to congratulate the heir to the throne, or be happy that his bride is the lively, handsome and serious woman she is, would assuredly put us in the second category.'

The news pages of that same day's papers, in reflecting their readers' values, again demonstrated the extraordinary, unwavering hold of the British monarchy on the imagination of its subjects. The appalling unemployment figures were, as Willie Hamilton feared, lost in the tide of 'The King and Di', right down to speculation by one fashion-page editor that the Queen-to-be might bite her nails. The attempted coup in Spain, ably fended off by King Juan Carlos, was as nothing to the Spencers' descent from Charles II's bastards – despite the obvious morals to be drawn about the comparative roles of Europe's constitutional monarchies in keeping would-be dictators at bay.

Mrs Thatcher had been informed by the Queen twenty-four hours earlier, and had travelled to the Palace to discharge her official duty, under the Royal Marriages Act of 1772, of granting Parliament's consent to the match. Now she departed in high spirits on a visit to her new political soulmate in Washington, President Ronald Reagan. There was no need for her or any of her supporters to spell out the truth behind Mr Hamilton's complaints: connivance or not, six months of royal celebration would ease her Government's mounting domestic problems. Just as England's victory in the 1966 World Cup football finals gave a boost in the polls to Harold Wilson's beleagured Labour Government, so Mrs

Thatcher's Conservatives could look to a patriotic surge among the people for renewed faith in the *status quo*.

The one figure in the drama whose *status quo* changed dramatically – as symbolically that day as it would in earnest in the coming years – was Lady Diana Spencer herself. The night before the announcement was the last she would spend in her Chelsea apartment, giggling with her flatmates over the morrow's dramatic news. At 11 am precisely, even as the statement flashed around the world from Buckingham Palace, a cohort of Special Branch detectives took up station outside her front door – and at her side. No longer would she be careering around London in the red Mini Metro which had become so well-known to the British press and public; that night it was a royal Rolls-Royce which carried her to join her fiancé for dinner with both their grandmothers at Clarence House. From that very night, a royal residence became her home. Already an apartment had been made ready for her use in the Queen Mother's residence, where she was duly installed after dinner that evening. 'Please,' she begged her flatmates as she said her tearful good-byes, 'please telephone me. I'm going to need you.'

It was all a rather brusque reminder of what Diana had let herself in for. She surrendered, that day, not just her anonymity, but her privacy, her independence, her freedom of movement, her job, her home, many of her friends – and, to a large extent, her identity. 'A woman not only marries a man,' her husband-to-be, a self-proclaimed opponent of Women's Liberation, once declared. 'She marries into a way of life – a job.' That, coming from him, was right royal understatement.

Few other women, these days, would marry on such terms, even for a £30,000 sapphire engagement ring with fourteen diamonds set in eighteen-carat white gold. But a look at Diana's upbringing, as everyone suddenly realized, made it seem that she, too, might almost have been born to this curious, unenviable fate.

CHAPTER TWO

Diana: The Girl Next Door

IN the end, after all the fandango – the flaps, the false starts, the furious flirtations – he fell for the girl, quite literally, next door. The woman chosen by Prince Charles to be his future Queen was born on the present Queen's estate at Sandringham, Norfolk, on 1 July 1961 – in Park House, the rambling country residence then rented by her father from the Royal Family. Her childhood playmates, over the shared garden wall, were Elizabeth II's younger sons, Prince Andrew and Prince Edward. The Queen herself she saw regularly enough to call 'Aunt Lilibet'. She first met Prince Charles when he was twelve – already named Prince of Wales, but not yet invested – and she was still in nappies.

'A lot of nice things happened to me when I was in nappies,' she was later to say, gently acknowledging the silver spoon lodged firmly in her infant mouth. Lady Diana Frances Spencer was the third daughter born to Edward John, Viscount Althorp, heir to the seventh Earl Spencer, and his wife Frances Ruth Burke Roche, younger daughter of the fourth Baron Fermoy. She could boast direct descent from the Stuart Kings of England, five times over from King Charles II - none of them, alas, on 'the right side of the blanket' - and once from James II. Her ancestors included Dukes of Bedford, Richmond, Abercorn, Marlborough and Grafton, and such illustrious English names as the Churchills, the Cumberlands, the Hertfords, the Waldegraves and – latterly more notorious – the Binghams, alias the Lucans. Her father was an equerry to King George VI, and later to his daughter Elizabeth II, whom he accompanied on her Coronation tour of Australia in 1954. Her mother was a lady-in-waiting to Queen Elizabeth The Queen Mother, and the daughter of one of her closest friends. One day, some eligible bachelor would find in Lady Diana a more than eligible bride.

'Johnny' Spencer had been hoping for a son and heir. The Althorps had seen one son die in infancy, and would three years later have another – aptly, as things turned out, named Charles – to ensure the direct male line of succession. But the birth of another daughter, for the eighth Earl Spencer-in-waiting, was at the time something of a disappointment.

Diana was a prim and rather proper little girl, more so even than her elder sisters Jane and Sarah, who were not themselves notably precocious. One reason was their upbringing on the fringes of the royal circle. The girls' grandmother, Lady Fermoy, was a lifelong friend of the Queen Mother, who was godmother to both Sarah and Jane; their father was himself a godson of King George V's widow, Queen Mary. The last arrival, young Charles, became godson to the present Queen, who enjoyed seeing the whole family during her several months each year at Sandringham. So Johnny saw to it that his offspring were bred as befitted, he felt, their station. While most other British children, however young, were in some way moulded by the 'Swinging Sixties', the Spencer brood learnt the old Edwardian virtues of knowing their place, speaking only when spoken to, behaving with deference to their elders, being seen little and heard less.

Diana was only six, and her younger brother just three, when one day her mother Frances suddenly 'disappeared'. That day in 1967, as a family retainer put it, Lady Althorp 'just wasn't there any more'. Sarah was twelve, Jane ten and their mother herself only thirty-one when she decided to put an end to her thirteen-year marriage to Johnny Spencer. The match had started in a blaze of glory - Frances had been the youngest bride this century to have married in Westminster Abbey, the young new Queen and her husband being among the guests - but it had since gone steadily downhill, reaching its acrimonious low point soon after Charles's birth in 1964. As in all such *pas devants les enfants* households, the children knew nothing, and were taken totally by surprise.

Diana was taken out of her King's Lynn nursery school and despatched to a

nearby preparatory school, Riddlesworth Hall, near Diss, where she distinguished herself more by effort than achievement. The rather gawky youngster,
said her headmistress, Elizabeth Ridsdale, was 'an entirely average' pupil. 'The
thing I remember most about her is that she was a perfectly ordinary, nice little
girl who was always kind and cheerful.' The judgment echoed that of Diana's
former governess, Gertrude Allen, who called her 'a conscientious girl. No, not
particularly bright ... but she did *try*.'

Like her 130 schoolmates, Diana donned the regulation grey shorts and
maroon jersey, and wore her hair 'off the collar'; but to her, perhaps, there was
especial significance in the school motto, 'Facing Forward', which appears to
be a bizarre aristocratic euphemism for stiff-upper-lipping your way through
good times and bad. For Diana, they were not too good. Perplexed by her
parents' sudden separation, and a maternal departure so precipitous that she
abandoned all four children to their father's care, she nevertheless had to spend
much of her school holidays flitting between the two. At Sandringham she still
saw the young Royals – though more, perhaps, of Prince Andrew than either of
his brothers – when they came round to swim in the Spencers' heated outdoor
pool.

Two years later, Diana had to endure the mockery of her schoolfriends as the
daily newspapers revelled in her parents' well-connected and bitterly contested
divorce case. Viscount Althorp sued his wife for adultery, with a wallpaper heir
named Peter Shand-Kydd, and lined up – for once the phrase is appropriate
– a veritable Who's Who of the British ruling classes in support of his claim
for custody of the children. He won a hard-fought victory, so painful to all
concerned that his former wife to this day still cannot bring herself to speak
of it.

That year, hard upon her defeat in the divorce courts, the former Viscountess
Althorp soon became plain Mrs Shand-Kydd. Diana and her siblings began a
regular vacation shuttle between Norfolk and their mother's new home in the
wilds of North-West Scotland, a white hillside manor house overlooking its own
1,000 acres, at Ardencaple on the Island of Seil, Argyllshire. After the Shand-
Kydds bought it in 1972, for a price said to be around £200,000, Diana's
mother quickly settled into a happy new domesticity, helping her husband on
their extensive sheep farm, and driving the fourteen miles north to Oban most
days to help out behind the counter of the newsagent's shop she owns in George
Street. As Diana's father, meanwhile, grew ever more morose in his unwonted
bachelordom, so their daughter grew closer to her mother, who through all the
travails and disruptions has remained the dominant influence in her life. When
Diana herself went through a not dissimilar public trauma twelve years later,

pursued by paparazzi hell-bent on cornering their future Queen, it was Mrs Shand-Kydd who flew to her side with advice and comfort, and who wrote an unprecedented letter of complaint to *The Times*, while her daughter's prospective in-laws looked on from the Palace in pained silence.

In 1975, when Diana was fourteen, her father became the eighth Earl Spencer on the death of his own father, Jack. Diana's little brother, eleven-year-old Charles, was now Viscount Althorp, and the family moved to its ancestral seat at Althorp (pronounced 'Altrup') in Northamptonshire. The 450-year-old stately pile, set in its own 1,500 acres, boasted a distinguished collection of paintings by such old masters as Gainsborough, Van Dyck and Rubens, but also conferred on the new Earl the less welcome inheritance of crippling death duties. Less than a year later, in the midst of dire financial difficulties, Johnny Spencer remarried – another divorcée, and a somewhat exotic one in the shape of Raine, Countess of Dartmouth, much-loved by gossip columnists as the colourful and outspoken daughter of Barbara Cartland. Miss Cartland, like her daughter, was rarely out of the society columns, promoting health foods and donning outrageous pink finery as she worked her way remorselessly towards her 300th romantic novel.

Raine Dartmouth's arrival on the scene at Althorp caused some dismay among the Spencer children. Her flamboyant style grated on them at first, and the sleepy halls of Althorp were not used to her brand of new-broom dynamism. But the place had to be spruced up, the death duties tackled, and Raine set about her task with a will. Neither children nor staff were too happy about the way she rejuvenated the estate, dismissing some of the long-standing family retainers and opening a shop for stately home visitors in the stable block. The Spencer children were reassured, however, by the obvious care and affection she lavished on their father.

Never was this more evident, or indeed vital, than in 1978, when Raine may be said to have saved her husband's life. In three years they had turned Althorp's finances around, and just a week before had thrown a party to celebrate its return to solvency at the bank. Then quite unexpectedly, one afternoon in the stable block, Johnny Spencer collapsed with a massive brain haemorrhage. Raine summoned a private ambulance and hurtled up the M1 with him to Northampton, where doctors told her that her fifty-five-year-old husband had little chance of surviving the night.

But somehow he did, and there followed a long fight to save his life, with Raine refusing to give up each time doctors told her there was no hope. She switched her husband from hospital to hospital, from specialist to specialist, determined that she would somehow pull him through. 'In a situation like that,'

Engagement day: Prince Charles has at last chosen his future Queen.

OVERLEAF LEFT The Earl of Chester meets members of the Cheshire Regiment.

OVERLEAF RIGHT Diana tries to get on with her work, but is trapped into that unfortunately revealing pose.

Charles about to play polo . . . and Diana looks loyally on.

LEFT The Prince of Wales in his 'mess dress' uniform as Commander-in-Chief of the Royal Regiment of Wales.

BELOW Highgrove House, the Gloucestershire country residence where Charles and Diana will make their home.

OPPOSITE The ninth Princess of Wales: a study by Lord Snowdon.

First public outing: Lady Diana asserts her independence in a daringly low-cut evening gown.

she said later, 'if you sit down and cry, you cry for yourself. The only thing I could do for him was to use my life and energy for his life.'

At last she turned in desperation to an old family friend, Bill Bentinck (now the Duke of Portland), the chairman of Bayer (UK). She had heard about a German-made 'miracle drug', Aslocillin, not yet tested or marketed in Britain, and asked Bentinck to use his connections to obtain some for her. He had what he called 'a bit of luck'. On contacting the head of his company's pharmaceuticals division, he learnt that they had at their laboratory in Haywards Heath, Sussex, a compound of the drug on which they were about to start clinical tests. It was unlicensed for sale or use in the United Kingdom, but Raine collected it herself from Victoria Station and managed to persuade her husband's doctors to try it.

Aslocillin, she now claims, saved Earl Spencer's life. After the initial haemorrhage he had contracted double pneumonia, an abscess on the lung which burst, and then double pneumonia again. This last infection was caused by a kind of bacterium, pseudomonas, which is resistant to normal drugs, so the Earl was very near death when the Aslocillin was administered. He soon showed remarkable signs of recovery.

With single-minded determination, his new wife coaxed and coddled him back to life. At times her interference earned her rebukes – 'there's nothing like a good row', she says, 'to cheer me up' – but in the end she was triumphantly vindicated. One afternoon she decided to play her still comatose husband a tape of Puccini's *Madam Butterfly*, and quite suddenly 'he just opened his eyes and was back'. It was not until December 1980 that her vindication, however, was truly complete: the drug Aslocillin finally completed its clinical trials and was permitted onto the British market.

Earl Spencer says he remembers little about his long period of intensive care, except the constantly encouraging voice of his wife. He is now restored to a remarkably full and active life, greeting the £1-a-head visitors to Althorp, even since the announcement of his daughter's distinguished engagement, and serving behind the counter of the wine store in the stable block. The only lingering trace of his illness is a slight hesitation in his speech. On 24 February, as the news of his daughter's betrothal spread around London, those outside the Palace who saw the bride's father arrive in his gold Rolls-Royce to join in the celebrations could have told nothing, from his appearance, about his recent brush with death.

By the time her father inherited Althorp, Diana had moved from Riddlesworth to another exclusive girls' school, £3,000-a-year West Heath, near Sevenoaks, Kent. Her friendship with the royal children continued in the school holidays. When Prince Charles wrote a children's story for his younger brothers in 1969 – eventually published in 1980, entitled *The Old Man of Lochnagar*, with illustrations by Sir Hugh Casson – he gave a copy to the eight-year-old girl-next-door as well. But while at West Heath it was Prince Andrew, just two years her senior, with whom Diana exchanged letters. There was much giggling in the dorm at the prospect, one day, of her perhaps enjoying a royal romance.

It was at West Heath that Diana met her closest friend, Carolyn Pride, now a student at the Royal College of Music and – until engagement day – one of her three flatmates at Coleherne Court in Chelsea. Some friendships still linger from her earlier days at Riddlesworth: Alexandra Lord, for instance, daughter of the land agent at Sandringham, and Caroline Harbord-Hammond, who works in the press department of Conservative Central Office.

The West Heath prospectus says that 'while some pupils go on to university, most train for practical careers'. Diana left at sixteen, with no practical career in mind, and no thoughts of university, having as always won more points for trying than for shining. Instead, she followed the well-worn path of well-born gels to a finishing school in Switzerland, the exclusive Château D'Oex near Montreux. One of the few unorthodox moments in her life came when she abruptly returned home after only six weeks; eager reporters searching for some skeleton in the Spencer locker could unearth only an acute bout of homesickness. She did at least use the time to learn a smattering of French, and to improve her prowess on the nursery slopes, both of which should come in handy in her new life with Prince Charles.

Like her sisters, but unlike their mother, Diana did not 'come out', nor has she since lived the typical London life now affected by most latter-day debutantes. After her father set her up in a £100,000 flat off the Old Brompton Road, with three flatmates paying rent directly to her, she was not to be found at those discos and night-clubs – Wedgies, Tokyo Joe's – in favour with the Sloane Rangers and their set. Her idea of a night out was to slip up the road to the ABC cinema, or to meet friends in a pub for 'a gin and tonic, please, with l-o-t-s of tonic'. A typical day in Diana's life, according to a friend, might be 'shopping at Harrods, perhaps for something for the flat. Or tea in Fortnum and Mason, before looking in the windows in Bond Street, or going for a wander among the fabrics in Liberty's.'

As much as this might stick in the gullet of Willie Hamilton MP, it should not be forgotten that Lady Diana did not, in fact, enjoy many 'ordinary days' during her sojourn as a London bachelor girl. Soon after arriving she found herself 'a proper sort of a job' helping Kay Seth-Smith and Vicky Wilson run the kindergarten school they had set up in a Pimlico church hall. The Young

England school was soon to become famous throughout the land, as hordes of press followed Diana to work there each day last autumn. There it was she was duped into the notorious 'see-through' photograph, when her agreement to pose for pictures resulted in her being manœuvred against the bright morning sunlight, wearing no slip beneath her diaphanous skirt. 'I don't want to be remembered', she said in heartfelt fashion next day, 'as the girl who didn't wear a petticoat.' By way of needless apology, she said to Prince Charles: 'Oh, my legs . . . like a Steinway piano.' Her gallant beau offered his sympathy for her embarrassment; but he also reassured her, as would have any young blood offered the chance, that her legs looked 'pretty damn good'.

Throughout the summer months of 1980, before the world discovered their romance, Diana told friends just that she was going out with a 'Charles Renfrew'. It was a happy revival of an old princely gambit, Baron Renfrew being one of the Prince of Wales's subsidiary titles; the future Edward VII, when Prince of Wales, travelled incognito under this name on his stormy tour of the United States in 1860. Prince Charles, while at university, once signed himself into a Cambridge club as Charlie Chester – which, as Charles, Earl of Chester, he had every right to do.

The friendship had blossomed into romance before the press finally tumbled to it. A series of secret meetings had to follow, once the courtship became public knowledge, and Charles's only fear was that Diana's ordeal by press would cause her, as it had several other girls, to abandon him. But centuries of Spencer phlegm, and Spencer involvement with the British Royal Family, had taught Diana where her true loyalties should lie. Charles need never have feared.

There was once a Lady Diana Spencer who did turn down a Prince of Wales, despite her family's best efforts to persuade her to accept him. She was born in 1708, the daughter of Charles Spencer, Earl of Sunderland, and of Lady Anne Churchill, one of the Marlboroughs of Blenheim. Diana's grandmother, the Duchess of Marlborough, was determined to arrange a match with the then Prince of Wales, Frederick Louis, son of George II and Queen Caroline, and later to become the father of the future King George III. But the Prince – a cultured but ill-starred man, now remembered mainly by his epitaph, 'Poor Fred, who was alive and is dead' – did not appeal at all to the young Lady Diana, who turned aside her grandmother's furious entreaties. She went off in a huff to marry the fourth Duke of Bedford instead, and lived only four more years, to die in childbirth.

That Diana, seven generations back, is an ancestral aunt of our heroine, whose own side of the family seems much better-trained to do royalty's bidding (see Appendix B). The Spencers first became a power in the land in the fifteenth

[35]

century, when one John Spencer purchased a sizeable chunk of Northamptonshire from the Abbot of Evesham. The family lived at Wormleighton in War-
wickshire, and had acquired their wealth through extensive sheep farming.
John Spencer is first mentioned in connection with Althorp in 1485, though the
purchase was not formally concluded until 1506. One hundred years and three
generations later, the family had become so wool-wealthy that titles were
inevitable. In the sixteenth century there were three Sir Johns and one Sir
William – all of them local luminaries, Knights of the Shire or Lieutenants of
the County, and all of them commemorated at Althorp by oak trees, and stones
dated 1566, 1588, 1602 and 1624.

The great-great-grandson of the original Sir John, Sir Robert Spencer, was
reputed to be the richest man – in terms of ready cash – in the kingdom. In
1603 King James I created him Baron Spencer of Wormleighton, and sent him
to invest the Duke of Wurtemburg with the Order of the Garter. The first
Baron Spencer commissioned a masque from Ben Jonson, performed before the
Queen of Denmark when she visited Althorp, and built the falconry (or 'stand-
inge') which can still be seen by weekend visitors today. He was a meticulous
economist, whose records of the numbers of 'suits of arras', furniture and plate
purchased for his home are still extant.

His son, the second Baron, married Lady Penelope Wriothesley, and was a
great entertainer: the family has preserved the bills for the enormous banquet
served at Althorp to King Charles I and Henrietta Maria in 1634. Henry, the
third Baron, married Lady Dorothy Sidney – the famous 'Sacharissa' of Edmund Waller's poems, the dedicatee of, among others, 'Go, lovely rose ...'.
Henry lent £10,000 to Charles I at the start of the Civil War; in return he was
created Earl of Sunderland, but died in action four months later at the Battle
of Newbury, aged only twenty-three. 'Sacharissa', a widow with four young
children, offered hospitality to the King when he was a prisoner at nearby
Holmby House, and it was at Althorp that Cornet Joyce attempted to abduct
him. The night before the Battle of Edgehill, Prince Rupert burnt down Wormleighton to prevent the rebel forces from fortifying it, so that Althorp became
the Spencer family's main residence from that day to this.

Henry's son Robert, who became the second Earl of Sunderland at the age
of two, proved both a cunning politician and the architect of Althorp's greatness
among English stately homes. A man of few scruples, he made himself indispensable to King Charles II, James II and William III in turn. All needed him,
but none of them trusted him, which is perhaps why he was despatched as
ambassador successively to Paris, Cologne and Madrid. According to the official
Althorp records, Robert was 'a first-rate man of business ...' but 'so extravagant

that he was compelled to be in office and to accept bribes from the French King to avoid bankruptcy'.

He was ambitious enough about Althorp to employ André le Nôtre, the gardener of Versailles, to lay out the grounds around a plan of magnificent avenues. His wife, Lady Anne Digby, – hated by Queen Anne, but renowned as one of the 'Windsor beauties' of Charles II's court – inherited many great paintings from her mother, the Countess of Bristol, to add to the collection acquired by Henry during his sojourns overseas (which included a period of exile in Holland). Althorp became so magnificent that it was much praised by the Grand Duke of Tuscany, and described for posterity by the great diarist, John Evelyn:

> The house or rather palace at Althorp is a noble uniform pile in form of a half H built of brick and freestone balustered and à la moderne; the hall is well, the staircase excellent; the rooms of state, galleries, office and furniture such as may become a great prince ...
>
> It is situate in the midst of a garden exquisitely planted and kept, and all this in a park walled in with hewn stone, planted with rows of walks of trees, canals, and fishponds and stored with game. And what is above all this, governed by a lady who without any show of solicitude keeps everything in such admirable order, both within and without, from the garret to the cellar, that I do not believe there is any in this nation, or in any other, that exceeds her in such exact order, without ostentation, but substantially great and noble. The meanest servant is lodged so neatly and cleanly; the service at the several tables, the good order and decency – in a word, the entire economy is perfectly becoming a wise and noble person.

'Such as may become a great prince ...': Evelyn, the inveterate gossip, would have enjoyed the fact that the furnishings of Althorp *will* now become a great prince – as well as being open to inspection by the general public at weekends.

In the early eighteenth century the Spencer family split, the senior branch becoming the Dukes of Marlborough (adding the name Churchill only in 1817) and the junior branch becoming the Earls Spencer (created in 1765). The first Earl – son of a renowned drunkard, tobacco pioneer and art connoisseur – married the coveted Georgiana Poyntz. He is now chiefly remembered for his saucy daughters, Henrietta, Lady Bessborough, who declined an affair with the Prince of Wales (the future George IV) and Georgiana, Duchess of Devonshire, who didn't. Georgiana's array of lovers also included the politician Charles James Fox, who is supposed to have begged her – without success – to marry him. Both girls, and their children, were painted by Reynolds and Gainsborough, thus adding to the Althorp collection. Their father's only other distinction, according to the family records, was as 'one of the pioneers of the modern manner of foxhunting'. The first Earl Spencer apparently 'brought the Pytchley Hounds up to a high state of efficiency'.

John Spencer also suffered from the terms of the will of his eccentric grandmother, the Duchess of Marlborough, who stipulated that her grandson and great-grandson must never – on pain of forfeiting the whole bequest – accept any 'employment' from the King other than a peerage. So the only political role Earl Spencer could enjoy was the financing of elections. Besides his obvious influence in Northamptonshire, he controlled the boroughs of St Albans and Okehampton; the election of 1768 is recorded to have lost him £120,000 – his only consolation being that both his opponents were ruined.

His son George, the second Earl Spencer, sensibly shunned such political extravagance, while representing Northamptonshire for twenty-eight years. He was colonel of the local Yeomanry for thirty-four, chairman of the Quarter Sessions and president of the local infirmary. At the same time, he became Lord Privy Seal, First Lord of the Admiralty, Pitt's ambassador to Vienna and Fox's Home Secretary. He was well enough in at court for both King George III and Queen Charlotte to become godparents to his daughter by Lady Lavinia Bingham, the society beauty immortalized by Reynolds's portraits of her. The Earl himself was a great collector of books, reputed to own 'the finest private library in Europe'. All the rooms at Althorp were so filled with books that the pictures had to be moved to the bedrooms.

His son John Charles, the third Earl Spencer, shared his father's enjoyment of both local and national politics, combined with a spot of foxhunting. He led the House of Commons during Grey's Reform Bill administration, became Chancellor of the Exchequer, and is said to have turned down the office of Prime Minister. The family history gives him short shrift, seemingly because he was 'devoid of all artistic feeling, his only contribution to the pictures at Althorp being twenty-seven portraits of his prize-winning shorthorn cattle'. His wife, Esther Acklom, died after giving birth to a stillborn son, so he was succeeded by his brother Frederick. The fourth Earl served as a naval officer and sensibly married another Poyntz, Elizabeth, who pleased the family by inheriting 'many works of art from Cowdray, her mother's home'. It is not mentioned that he was meanwhile Lord Chamberlain, with the rank of Rear-Admiral in the Navy.

His son, John Poyntz, fifth Earl Spencer, followed his great-grandfather as First Lord of the Admiralty, adding such distinctions as Keeper of the Privy Seal, 'Groom of the Stole' to Prince Albert, and two stints as Lord-Lieutenant of Ireland – during which he vainly attempted to persuade Queen Victoria to give his office to her son, the Prince of Wales. His wife, Charlotte Seymour, was a society beauty so renowned as to be known as 'Spencer's Fairy Queen' while they held court in Dublin.

John was succeeded by his half-brother, Charles Robert, the sixth Earl, who kept up the family tradition by becoming Lord Chamberlain to both King Edward VII and his son, King George V. He was succeeded in 1922 by his eldest son, Albert Edward John, who three years earlier had married Lady Cynthia Hamilton, daughter of the third Duke of Abercorn. Their son, Edward John, is now the eighth Earl Spencer, and father of the new Princess of Wales.

Lady Diana's other ancestors include the seventeenth-century pornographic poet, Lord Rochester; Britain's first Prime Minister, Robert Walpole, a major figure in the lives of two of her predecessors as Princess of Wales; the Earl of Lucan who saved the Heavy Brigade from the fate of the Light Brigade; and that Bishop Trelawny immortalized in the lines:

> And shall Trelawny die?
> Here's twenty thousand Cornish men
> Will know the reason why!

The Spencers, in short, are more English than the Royal Family. 'The real aristocracy in this country is that which existed before the Industrial Revolution, when lots of people who owned factories were given titles,' says Harold Brooks-Baker, managing director of *Debrett's Peerage*. 'There are only about 150 families in that category, and the Spencers are well towards the top of them.... There is nobody in her family of great importance, but they are nice people who live in beautiful houses and have the good fortune to be related to almost every member of the aristocracy.' Genealogists, on these occasions, seem able to stretch the line almost to the crack of doom. Prince Charles, for instance, has been shown to be a descendant of all the English Kings and Queens who had issue, save the Stuarts – whom Lady Diana will now bring back to the royal line – and from such disparate historical figures as Charlemagne and Genghis Khan, Shakespeare and Count Dracula, El Cid and George Washington. Washington, albeit the first, is the only American president directly linked to Charles; Diana, by contrast, can claim connections with no fewer than seven, from John Adams to Franklin Delano Roosevelt.

Diana and Charles, through King Henry VIII, are sixteenth cousins once removed. Through William Cavendish, third Duke of Devonshire (1698-1755), a descendant of James I, they are seventh cousins once removed. By recent royal standards, this is scarcely rash inter-breeding. But the fact that Diana's parents are divorced would until recently have disqualified her from consideration. It is a mark of Elizabeth II's shrewd overhaul of royal morality, during her twenty-eight years on the throne, that the Spencer divorce was never an issue. Divorce may be a commonplace of the contemporary world, but until that of Princess Margaret from Lord Snowdon in 1978 the monarch, in her titular role as 'Defender of the Faith', felt unable to acknowledge it as such. Divorce had never been allowed to encroach so near the throne since the headstrong days of King Henry VIII. For all that, Earl Spencer's second wife, Raine, the former Countess of Dartmouth, has not been permitted to accompany him to Buckingham Palace on his visits to the Queen since the engagement was announced. Raine will also take a back seat to Diana's mother, Mrs Shand-Kydd, on the wedding day itself.

But to be eligible to become the forty-eighth Queen of England, the first Princess of Wales for seventy years and the first English girl to marry an heir to the throne for more than three hundred, Lady Diana did have to endure one signally embarrassing public morality test. It was a curious manifestation of late twentieth-century morals that Diana had to be publicly accepted as – even publicly pronounced to be – unblemished, or *intacta*: not to mince words, a virgin. As Robert Lacey, author of *Majesty*, the best-selling biography of Queen Elizabeth II, put it to *Newsweek* magazine: 'The family put pressure on Charles to find a girl with no past, and there aren't that many nineteen-year-old virgins available.' Poor Diana, therefore, had to stand by and suffer the indignity as her uncle, Lord Fermoy, assured the press of her unsullied reputation. *Private Eye*, the satirical magazine, had been making insinuations about Diana's former friendship with a young Army officer and Old Etonian. In stepped His Lordship to defend his niece's honour. 'Lady Diana, I can assure you,' he intoned to an astonished gathering of journalists, 'has never had a lover. There is no such thing as her ever having had a past.'

So, that final hurdle o'ercome, Diana was at last acceptable as the first English-born bride of a potential King since Anne Hyde, elder daughter of the first Duke of Clarendon, married the future King James II in 1659. But Lady Anne died in 1671, fourteen years before James's accession to the throne, and he subsequently married an Italian Catholic Princess, Mary Beatrice of Modena. So Lady Diana, should she become Queen, will be the first English-born Queen Consort since the reign of Henry VIII, four of whose six wives were English. Elizabeth Bowes-Lyon, now Queen Elizabeth The Queen Mother, was Scottish-born, and anyway had no expectation of becoming Queen when she married the Duke of York, younger brother of the Prince of Wales, in 1923. Edward VIII and George VI's father, King George V, married Princess Mary of Teck, daughter of a German Duke, who had previously been betrothed to his unfortunate elder brother, Prince Eddy. Edward VII's Princess and Queen,

Alexandra, was the daughter of King Christian ix of Denmark, and his mother, Queen Victoria, married a German, Prince Albert – as did all her Hanoverian ancestors back to George i in 1714. Her predecessor, Queen Anne, married the son of the King of Denmark; and her predecessor, Queen Mary, married William of Orange, who could claim to be only one-quarter English.

Said Mr Charles Kidd, editor of *Debrett's Peerage*: 'Many royal marriages in the past were dynastic, as with the Hanoverians marrying the Germans, or they were to help enforce treaties, as when Charles ii married Catherine of Braganza.' The former editor, Mr Patrick Montague-Smith, said there could be 'no more noble family for Prince Charles to marry into' than the Spencers (family motto: 'God defend their right').

Apart from regally acceptable genes, Lady Diana brings to Prince Charles's life a mutual love of the outdoors, of salmon fishing, of skiing, of music (she plays the piano, and may encourage him to buy himself another cello), and of laughter. She does not smoke; he detests the habit. She does not drink much; nor does he, though he can make short work of a gin-and-tonic at the end of a long day, and will share a pre-prandial martini with his parents. She dyes her eyelashes, which, as far as we know, he does not. She does not – whisper it at your peril in royal circles – much like horses, having fallen off one in her youth, and now being somewhat wary of the creatures. Her future husband, as we know, does like horses; and Lady Diana was sufficiently supportive, four days before the announcement of their engagement, to share his grief as he cradled the head of his dying steed, Allibar, after a fall. Journalists have hitherto failed to come up with much in the way of sensation from her impeccable, and short-lived, past – the fact that she was once thrown fully clothed into a swimming pool being deemed to merit the whole of the front page of the *Sunday Mirror*. The most delightful manifestation hitherto of her sense of humour, and her refusal to be dazzled by matters royal, is that when accompanying the Prince of Wales to one of his early steeple-chasing ventures at Ludlow, she backed her future husband for a place, rather than a win.

She is known to enter into the Royal Family's holiday pastime of charades with more enthusiasm and less self-consciousness than Princess Anne's husband, Mark Phillips. She was, in the later stages of her romance with Charles, subjected to a discreet gynaecological check-out, to ensure that she could bear him heirs. She is, in the words of her redoubtable step-grandmother, Barbara Cartland – author in 1979 of a torrid tome entitled *Bride To The King* – 'purity itself'.

In her new role as Princess of Wales, Diana may see rather less of her elder sister Sarah, now twenty-five, and the wife of Old Etonian landowner Neil

McCorquodale. She will probably see rather more, however, of her next sister Jane, twenty-four, wife of Robert Fellowes, once a member of Prince Charles's staff, now an assistant private secretary to the Queen. Many of her other friends, alas, she will be forced to leave behind her, unsuitable as they will be deemed for royalty's innermost circles. She will have to give up much else besides.

She will never be able to call her husband by his Christian name in public. Wherever she goes, she will be expected to walk one pace behind him. She will be able to arrive nowhere unannounced, nor to walk down a street without months of preparation by scores of people. She has, in short, agreed to make herself a piece of public property.

The consolations are considerable. Her future security, and that of her children, is assured. Her husband, who already has a handsome income, will in time become one of the richest men in the world. Yet he and his family will continue to live at public expense. Diana will never have to wash her own dishes, change her children's nappies or fret about their education, worry about her mortgage or having nothing new to wear. She'll have a choice of seven or eight palaces to call home. Her children won't have to bite their nails about meetings with the school careers officer.

But the price she must pay for all this is unenviable. She will meet princes and potentates, but she must also make polite conversation to interminable mayors at interminable dinner parties. She must take a passionate interest in Girl Guides and Women's Institutes. She must cut many a ribbon, plant many a tree, lay many a foundation stone, launch a few ships. She must declare things open, declare things closed. It must all be done with an unwavering smile, and never a word out of place, never a name forgotten. She must never, but never, appear anything other than radiant, gracious and content. In the months preceding her wedding, she has already received a crash course in these and other aspects of 'becoming royal' from her future husband's grandmother, Queen Elizabeth The Queen Mother.

Prince Charles's choice of Lady Diana as his bride is, indeed, interpreted in royal circles as a 'victory' for the Queen Mother over the forces of the late Lord Mountbatten, who had always hoped Charles would marry one of his granddaughters, the Knatchbull girls. In the wake of his death at the hands of IRA terrorists, there was in fact a brief courtship between the Prince of Wales and Amanda Knatchbull, daughter of Lord and Lady Brabourne, at whose Caribbean holiday home, on the island of Eleuthera, Charles had spent several vacations. But their mutual affection never blossomed into love.

Close as he has been throughout his life to both the Queen Mother and Mountbatten, it is an annoyance to Charles that his choice should be so portrayed. But the reasons are not hard to find. Both Lady Diana's grand-mothers and four of her great-aunts were, or still are, attendants at Queen Elizabeth's 'court'.

Countess Spencer (1897–1972) was a Lady of the Bedchamber, and Ruth, Lady Fermoy, Diana's other grandmother, has been a Woman of the Bedcham-ber (fine distinction) since 1960. Lady Delia Peel (born 1889) was an Extra Woman of the Bedchamber; her sister, Lady Lavinia Spencer (died 1955), was an Extra Lady-in-Waiting to the Queen Mother when she was Duchess of York, and she in her turn was Lady Lavinia's bridesmaid. Lady Katharine Seymour (born 1900) is another Extra Woman of the Bedchamber, and Diana's fourth great-aunt, The Dowager Duchess of Abercorn, is the Queen Mother's Mistress of the Robes. At the wedding, as *The Times* pointed out, 'she will have as many Spencers around her as the bride'.

All of which is rather appropriate, as those who know both ladies say that Diana shares many of the characteristics of the former Elizabeth Bowes-Lyon, born the daughter of the fourteenth Earl of Strathmore. It is not merely a question of being shyer, and less worldly, than other girls her age. It is a matter of providing unfailing support, at moments of stress, to a man who's going to be in dire need of it. The Queen Mother has known Diana 'since she was so high', and she has told friends she takes the comparison as a high compliment. Coming from her – whose eightieth birthday in 1980 had Britain at her feet – that is in turn the highest of compliments.

Diana, what's more, may well one day find herself filling the peculiar niche carved in the public's affection by the present Queen Mother. Given the longevity of the females of the House of Windsor, she may well outlive her husband, like Queen Elizabeth, Queen Mary and Queen Alexandra before her, to add an extra dimension to her offspring's inheritance of the throne. She may not wish to think of it now, but it is a fate for which she may look to her grandmothers' and great-aunts' closest friend for inspiration.

CHAPTER THREE

Charles: Monarch in the Making

O N his thirtieth birthday in 1978, after the razzle-dazzle celebrations in Buckingham Palace and around the country, the Prince of Wales told his staff that he had three priorities for the decade ahead: to find out more about the nation over which he would one day reign, to do more work abroad as an unofficial salesman for British industry, and to find the nation and the Commonwealth its future Queen.

It was the end of a period of drift, an unhappy one in which Prince Charles had come to resent the pervasive popular perception that he was an ageing playboy without a job. For one thing, he hated growing old; Peter Pan-like, he refused to sanction any interviews, TV programmes or public celebrations of the fact that he had reached thirty, major milestone though it was as perhaps his half-way point to the throne. For another, he had been working harder than ever before in his life.

True, he had no clearly identifiable public role – a perennial problem for Princes of Wales, for whom no allowance is made in the British Constitution.

Since leaving the Services he had been photographed almost entirely in such off-duty pursuits as playing polo, falling off racehorses, jumping out of aeroplanes and kissing pretty girls. It was no wonder his public was growing disenchanted. But he had chaired the Queen's Silver Jubilee Trust the previous year, which had raised £16 million – an astonishing sum from a nation of less than sixty million people. Now he was in charge of administering that money, as well as the several other trusts and charities he had founded under his own name. He had embarked on a series of visits to government and industry around Britain, and continued his travels as a goodwill ambassador abroad. 'I work bloody hard right now, and will continue to,' he said in a sudden public outburst.

He was also, rather self-consciously, trying to assert his independence. His life so far had been very carefully ordered for him. Its course had been charted by his parents and their advisers; Charles had been consulted, more so than any previous heir in history, but scarcely at the helm. Now he conspicuously began to make his own decisions. He appointed himself a new private secretary, Edward Adeane, after the departure of Squadron-Leader David Checketts, who had stewarded his young master's life since his early teenage schooldays in Australia. His assistant private secretary, Oliver Everett, was a dynamic young man brought over by the Foreign Office to organize his programme of familiarization with sundry British institutions. Both his press officer and his other more junior aides were all in their thirties, as were his personal staff: equerry, valets, secretarial team. The breeze of youth was at last sweeping down the musty, university-like corridors of Buckingham Palace, where so much of the past was preserved around him, as if in aspic. But there was still something missing.

The Palace has never been a master of the art of public relations, preferring to hire diplomats who regard their job as the suppression of news rather than slick advertising types intent on making headlines and reshaping the royal image. But it did not need Madison Avenue to tell the Prince of Wales and his staff that he should put his third priority first. What he needed most, for the benefit of his public popularity, his professional usefulness and his private contentment, was a wife.

He had become a very solitary figure, often dining alone in his three-room suite at the Palace in front of the TV, and cocooned in a tight circle of friends with a limited interest in much apart from polo, grouse shooting and the *status quo*. The chores, frustrations and sheer tedium of his life were beginning to outweigh its considerable perks. Shortly before his birthday, a Qantas air hostess had settled into conversation with him and, instead of trotting out the usual star-struck platitudes, had said: 'God, what a rotten, boring job you've got!'

When he told the story to the Callaghan Cabinet, at a private dinner in his honour at Chequers, they all laughed politely. 'But no,' wailed the Prince in desperation, 'you don't understand what I mean. She was right!'

The anecdote ends with one of the most senior politicians present, deep in his cups, tweaking the heir to the throne gently on the cheek and saying: 'Well, you shouldn't have taken the job, then, should you?' The joke, for once, was on Charles. But perhaps the biggest psychological hurdle he has had to overcome is the fact that he did *not* choose his unenviable lot, that it was a quirk of genetic fate which bundled him feet-first into what has been called 'a comfortable form of inherited imprisonment'. He needed, above all, someone to share his solitary confinement.

He was, on his thirtieth birthday, the oldest unmarried Prince of Wales since James Stuart, the Old Pretender, in 1718 – apart, of course, from his great-uncle the Duke of Windsor, who abandoned the throne in 1936 for 'the woman I love'. Charles regarded it as something of an achievement to have reached the age of thirty unmarried. It broke all recent royal precedents. His parents married when his father was twenty-six, his mother twenty-one. His grandfather, King George VI, married at twenty-seven; his great-grandfather, George V, at twenty-eight; his great-great-grandfather, Edward VII, at twenty-one. Of his own generation of the Royal Family, his sister Anne married at twenty-three, and his cousins the Dukes of Kent and Gloucester at twenty-five and twenty-seven.

Of those Princes of Wales who became Kings of England, only Henry V and Charles II were unmarried at thirty, and each of them remained so only two more years. Now, by marrying at thirty-two, Prince Charles is matching up to the history of his office. His wedding comes – after more than a decade of unremitting pressure from press and public, and to a lesser extent from his family and friends – as in many ways a merciful release.

In recent years, his hunt for a bride has come to haunt Prince Charles. He had come close to marriage in his early twenties, but had then been about to embark on a sustained stint in the Services which would keep him away from home for the best part of six years. By the time he emerged from the Navy, at the age of twenty-eight, he was of a mind to prolong his independence. Although thirty was looming on the horizon – the age at which, to his eternal regret, he once said 'a chap like me' should get married – there seemed no particular hurry. He had two younger brothers to ensure the succession, and perhaps another thirty years before he inherited the throne. For the first time in his life, moreover, this fundamentally shy figure, still in some ways young for his years, publicly noted for his weak chin and jug ears, found he had developed an extraordinary power over women – a kind of *ex officio* sex appeal. It took him by surprise, and he began rather to enjoy it.

For the next few years the Prince of Wales, wherever he went, played the role of a besieged sex symbol. Girls would giggle and scream at his approach as if he were a pop star, lunge forth with kisses as if he were a matinée idol, fight to touch him as if he were divine. He led the life of the world's most eligible bachelor, romantically linked with some of the world's most glamorous women. On the surface, in an awkward sort of way, he seemed to enjoy it – unless fighting off the public embraces of married women, such as the American TV star Farrah Fawcett, or those with otherwise 'unsuitable' lifestyles, such as the film star Susan George. But at heart, he was always looking for his oft-mentioned English rose (so oft-mentioned that he once caused a diplomatic incident by forgetting to admit the possibility of a Welsh rose), someone who would be as privately loving and supportive as she would be publicly loyal, discreet and conscientious. There just weren't many of them, from the 'right' sort of families, about.

The other restrictions on his choice were daunting. He could not, since the 1689 Bill of Rights (enshrined in the 1701 Act of Settlement, by which the present Royal Family's claim to the throne is legally established) marry a Roman Catholic. At the height of the rumours about Princess Marie-Astrid of Luxembourg, to whom the *Daily Express* 'officially' engaged him in 1977, he told a friend, 'I just can't do that. If I marry her, I'm dead. I'm not going to sacrifice myself on that altar.' He had followed his mother's wishes by travelling secretly to Brussels to look the Princess over, but no amount of meetings between archbishops and popes, politicians and cardinals, could make even the specu-lation feasible. Hovering in the wings, meanwhile, cries of 'Popery' on their lips, were Mr Enoch Powell MP and other members of the Ulster Unionist Party, whose anxious noises of dissent were still continuing in the summer of 1980, as Charles fished contentedly at Balmoral with his latest lady-love, Diana Spencer.

Nor could he marry without the consent of the sovereign, his mother, or both Houses of Parliament, as stipulated by the Royal Marriages Act of 1772 – initiated, ironically enough, by Charles's hero King George III, in an attempt to stop his wayward sons marrying mere English roses. There could be no question, given his future position as titular head of the Church of England and 'Defender of the Faith', of his marrying a divorcée; in this respect, if in few others, the public display of family morality expected of the British Royals has remained unchanged since the abdication crisis of 1936. Elizabeth II has gently eased the monarchy into the latter-half of the twentieth century, social values and all, as witnessed by the fact that in 1955 she forbade her sister to marry a divorced man, yet twenty-five years later permitted her to divorce the man she had married in his stead. But there were universal cries of dismay when Charles allowed himself, in the summer of 1979, to be seen in the company of Jane Ward, a chirpy, talkative divorcée who had just become secretary of his polo club. Fortunately for all concerned, Jane soon ruled herself out of consideration by breaking Rule Number 1A: Never talk to the press.

The Prince was compelled, as we have seen, to search for a girl 'without a past'; and, as has been less publicized, to marry someone young enough to bear him children – the heirs of the Royal House of Windsor – without the remotest possible gynaecological risk. Non-Catholic, non-divorced European princesses were as thin on the ground as unblemished, blue-blooded British girls in their late teens or early twenties. Many of the available candidates were beginning to give up on him and marry his friends, or other members of the British ruling or moneyed classes, while they still had the chance. 'Whenever I give a dinner party these days,' he complained to a friend, 'everyone I ask seems to be getting married.' 'You'd better get on with it, Charles,' his worldly-wise father would chide him, 'or there won't be anyone left.'

Elizabeth II, although she has never specifically forbidden her son to marry a commoner, has always impressed upon him her wish that the 'purity' of the Blood Royal be preserved, or even enhanced, by a marriage into one of the 'great' British or European families. If not someone of royal birth, then his bride should ideally be a girl who brought good genes to his lineage as much as contentment to his hearth. More his mother than his Queen, in private as in public, Elizabeth restrained herself from increasing the pressure on Charles by adding her own voice to the chorus of impatience. But he was aware of the public's dismay, and of the increasingly wild rumours: that he would eventually go the way of the Duke of Windsor, that he was interested only in married women, even that he was homosexual. Something, as the last Prince of Wales once famously said, had to be done.

As the British and European press accounted for many a forest in its attempts to make his choice for him, there lurked in the outer shadows of Prince Charles's life the one girl who might well have been dreamt up by a computer dating firm to meet all the many strict requirements he had marked on his card. Once he had named her, and the British public had offered its enthusiastic blessing, it seemed suddenly as if there had never been any question of his marrying anyone else.

Charles thus chalked up yet another in the long line of royal 'firsts' in his young life: he became the first Prince of Wales in history not to consider, let alone settle for, an arranged marriage. He had, to put it mildly, taken his time over his choice; Lady Diana, for her part, had at least given the impression of allowing herself an appropriately breathless pause before making hers. There was, at first, the appearance that this might be as much a marriage of necessity as of true hearts and minds; but it was never a marriage of convenience. Public euphoria, the while, has a way of dispelling all such first impressions. Within a year or two, the young couple will appear in the eyes of their adoring public to have been blissfully married for ever and a day.

The other royal precedents in Prince Charles's history began before he was born, when his grandfather, King George VI, announced that he was abolishing the ancient custom whereby the Home Secretary had personally to attend and verify the birth of a royal heir. Crowds lingered outside Buckingham Palace throughout that rainy Sunday, 14 November 1948, until it was announced that at 9.14 pm the Princess Elizabeth had been 'safely delivered of a Prince'. A chain of beacons was lit across the land, and the fountains in Trafalgar Square turned blue for a week.

The child was barely three years old, and his parents just settled into Clarence House, when George VI died at the age of fifty-six. Prince Charles of Edinburgh was suddenly Duke of Cornwall and heir apparent; legally, he had come of age. His mother, who had hoped for many more years of undisrupted family life before inheriting the throne, was suddenly busy all day – in a role for which she was so unprepared as often, in those early days, to be reduced to tears. She did, however, persuade the then Prime Minister, Winston Churchill, to put back the hour of his weekly audience so she could be with her children at bedtime.

Like Bertie, Prince of Wales, before him, Charles had the prospect of waiting more than half a century to inherit the throne. Unlike Bertie, however, he had understanding and sympathetic parents, well aware of the difficulties of so long an apprenticeship, and prepared to learn from the mistakes of their forebears. The new Elizabethan era, so warmly hailed by Churchill, was one of cosy domestic monarchy, the First Family giving its people unprecedented glimpses into its private life by way of authorized books and TV films. Prince Charles became the first heir apparent in British history to go to school with other children – albeit private schools for the sons of the privileged – and eventually the first to win himself a university degree.

He had the advantage of a father with a 'normal', if disrupted, education, and a mother who knew that her own, at the hands of Palace tutors, had been woefully inadequate. Prince Philip, in those uncertain early years, tended to win most of the family arguments, and so it was no coincidence that the schools eventually attended by Charles were those attended by his father before him. After a brief stint as a day boy at Hill House School in London, mightily disrupted by the press, he was despatched as a boarder to Cheam, in Hampshire, and then further afield to Gordonstoun, in the inaccessible wilds of Scotland.

They were not always happy years, but he has decided in retrospect that they were more than worthwhile. (There is every reason to suppose that Prince Charles will wish his own sons to tread the same, now well-worn, royal path.) The heir to the throne was at a disadvantage in the peculiarly brutal, amoral world of the British public schoolboy, however much good it may have done him to polish his own shoes, make his own bed and take his turn to empty the dustbins – just as if, as the society columnists kept simpering, he were a 'normal' child. His two terms away from Gordonstoun, at Geelong grammar school in Australia, were by far the happiest, the least disrupted and most formative, of his schooldays. 'I went out to Australia with a boy,' said David Checketts, 'and returned with a man.'

As he grew up, the Prince was taught to understand, but not abuse, his rank. If he left a door open, his father told footmen he must shut it himself. If rude to Palace servants, he was spanked and told to apologize; if he threw snowballs at them, they were encouraged to throw a few back. Once, at Sandringham, he was sent back out into the grounds to find a dog lead he had lost. 'Dog leads', the Queen told her son, 'cost money.'

Elizabeth II became the first British monarch to insist that her children should *not* bow and curtsey to her. At Cambridge Charles lived in college, whereas his grandfather and great-great-grandfather before him had lived in splendid isolation on the city outskirts, their tutors travelling to them, and their fellow students being expected to stand up whenever they entered the room. Neither George VI or Edward VII risked taking a final exam; Charles did, and won himself a reassuringly average second-class degree.

Reluctantly, and against the wishes of his university mentor, Lord Butler, he again took two terms out from his normal course of education – this time to attend the University College of Wales, Aberystwyth, as a gesture to his uncertain subjects in the principality of Wales. It was the summer of 1969, and the date of his investiture at Caernarvon Castle – symbol of the English usurpation of Welsh sovereignty – was drawing near. Charles thus became the first English Prince of Wales in the 668-year history of the office to take the trouble to learn a bit of Welsh. (Many had never even bothered to go near the place.)

The investiture was billed as the climax of his preparation for entry into public life, the moment for Charles to carve himself a lasting niche in the public consciousness. It was the culmination of a carefully calculated two-year plan for the marketing of a Prince of Wales, devised by Checketts, a former public relations man, at the Queen's specific behest. But the timing proved to be unfortunate. It was the last year of the first Wilson Government, a period of much-resented public austerity, which coincided with the rise of a fierce strain of nationalism around the principality. With terrorist bombs going off all over Wales, threats being made daily to the Prince's life, and the Government turning away all suggestions that the ceremony be called off, the lavish mini-coronation of the Prince of Wales looked like being the first serious mistake made by the Queen on his behalf.

But it turned out to be something of a personal triumph – thanks largely to the skills with which Charles himself squared up to his first major ordeal by public adulation. An Eistedfodd speech in Welsh had his adopted nation at his feet, drowning out the dissenting murmurs of Plaid Cymru, with the Mayor of Caernarvon standing up to declare: 'That wasn't just a boy. That was a Prince. You could have put a suit of armour on him and sent him off to Agincourt.' More significantly, perhaps, he had given his first series of newspaper, radio and TV interviews, in which he emerged for the first time as a relaxed, witty, likeable figure, able to laugh with anyone else at the absurdities of his royal life. He founded a series of trusts for charitable, youth and environmental work around Wales and the rest of the United Kingdom, which have since spread their work around the Commonwealth. He began to travel abroad. Suggestions from the highest circles that he 'clinched' an £11 million export deal in Brazil may be unconvincing, but in Japan he certainly did persuade Sony to build a factory in the Rhondda – and was able, two years later, to open it himself, bringing much-needed employment to one of Wales's most depressed regions. At last, to himself and those around him, he was feeling his way towards a role in which he could prove himself, and be seen to prove himself, useful.

In 1936, at the time of Edward VIII's abdication, an opinion poll showed that fully half the country thought it a good opportunity to do away with the monarchy. In 1969, on the eve of Charles's investiture, another showed that seventy per cent whole-heartedly approved of the institution. By Charles's thirtieth birthday in 1978, and an Opinion Research Centre survey for *Woman* magazine, the figure had risen to eighty-six per cent. Eighteen months later, early in 1980, a Marplan poll for *Now* magazine named Prince Charles, for the first time, the most popular member of the Royal Family. Respondents were asked to name 'the two most likeable members of the Royal Family'; Prince Charles clocked up seventy per cent, compared to only forty-six for the Queen and thirty per cent for the Queen Mother – a remarkable reversal of the usual ratings. Prince Philip received a twenty-one per cent vote of public approval, Prince Andrew eleven, Princess Alexandra nine, Princess Margaret three and poor Captain Mark Phillips just one.

The restoration of the monarchy from its hour of greatest trauma, less than fifty years ago, may in time be seen to resound as much to Prince Charles's credit as to that of his mother and grandfather. Prince Charles, moreover, has worked hard for his increasing public popularity, unlike his two immediate predecessors, who both entered their thirties regarded by their future subjects as little more than globe-trotting dilettantes.

The future Edward VII was a highly unpopular figure for dragging the monarchy into a divorce scandal, but he spent his thirtieth birthday gravely ill, apparently dying of typhoid. His unexpected recovery six weeks later proved how the institution oft outshines the man; the nation, surprised at its own fickleness, found itself calling for a day of national rejoicing. The future Edward VIII, by contrast, spent his thirtieth birthday planning a private trip to America. No trade deals for him: it was a constant round of galas and parties, which had his staff wondering where he had got to each night, and his father in a rage at such American headlines as 'Prince Gets In With The Milkman'. Six years later, he was to meet Mrs Simpson.

If the present Prince of Wales lacks the lustre of his immediate predecessors, it at times seems just as well. He may not be a leader of fashion, as were both Bertie and 'David'; he may not have Edward VIII's knack of putting people at their ease in the royal presence, or Edward VII's instinct for the grand gesture. But none of this would bother him. 'If people think me square,' he has said, deliberately choosing a somewhat dated epithet, 'then I am happy to be thought square.' Having lived all his life in a world of adults, and extremely genteel adults at that, he has developed a profoundly traditional sense of values, and a driving, almost obsessive sense of duty. He will not, like his great-great-grandfather, be dragging the monarchy into the courts; nor will he, like his great-uncle, be found reneging on his promises. If Charles says 'Something must be done' – as, on occasion, he has – we can be rather more confident that it will be.

Playing a strictly non-political role is one of the great frustrations of his life, but there need be no such inhibitions in private. Charles has for some years now already received his 'red boxes' of state and Cabinet papers, and is not averse to sending his views on matters of the day to the Prime Minister. He formed a particularly close friendship with James Callaghan, who let him sit in on the occasional Cabinet meeting, and who has confessed to being outsmarted by Charles on the small print of various Cabinet memoranda. The Prince meets politicians of all hues regularly, in the extreme confidentiality of Privy Council terms, and speaks his mind (which tends to the conservative).

There is a formidable amount of paperwork in his job, and the Prince is none too keen on it, at times downright sloppy. Documents sent to him for signature are invariably returned at the last minute, often late; speeches tend to be delivered for typing just when everybody is ready to go home. (He has the benefit of a secretarial staff and a photocopier on the royal train when last-minute panics beset excursions out of town.) He has one part-time speechwriter, but the finished product is always his own work.

Part of his excuse for this dilatoriness, often justifiably, is pressure on his time. The journalists around Prince Charles, who spend most of their lives living his, divide into two heated camps on this issue: those who recite his myriad honorary positions and mundane chores, and who find it difficult to keep up with the cracking pace he sets on tour; and those who moan about his long annual holidays at Balmoral and Sandringham, Deauville and Iceland, Klosters and the Caribbean. When one in the latter camp insisted on seeing the Prince's large red appointments diary (which he fills in himself, leaving his staff to make the arrangements), he was shown a particularly full November week; on complaining that Tuesday afternoon seemed free, he had a red box overflowing with paperwork thrown at him by an exasperated Oliver Everett.

When the Prince can relax, his two favourite pastimes are strangely incongruous: riding horses and listening to 'good' music (notably opera, of which he is now beginning to expand his rather thin knowledge). He has taken with a vengeance to steeplechasing – 'the sport of kings' – and not always with the happiest of results. In March 1981 he had two nasty falls, at Sandown Park and at Cheltenham, thus reviving the old debate which had so irritated the last Prince of Wales in the 1920s: should the heir to the throne be permitted to risk his neck like this? The future Edward VIII had become so reckless a steeplechaser that his father, King George V, called in two successive Prime Ministers, Stanley Baldwin and Ramsay MacDonald, to try and talk him out of it. They eventually succeeded, though the Prince was extremely annoyed. Prince Charles seems intent on continuing to ride in National Hunt races, despite a consensus among the experts that he is not, alas, quite up to it. 'He just isn't good enough,' said a Cheltenham official after the Prince's second fall in five days. 'He should stick to point-to-points, which are of a much lower standard. He is trying to compete at the very highest level, with few skills to match. He shouldn't take part in races of this calibre.' Said the man from Ladbroke's, Mr Mike Dillon: 'You get sympathy if you fall off once ... but not if it becomes a habit.'

After the second fall, even the Prince himself admitted it was his – not the horse's – mistake, adding: 'It's a bloody nuisance ... now I've got to go home and face them all again, I suppose.' When he did, the Queen again tried to talk him out of taking such risks – as she once had, five years before, when he insisted on flying helicopters and jet aircraft during his spell in the Navy and RAF. On that occasion, she was less successful, though the Prince was never allowed to realize his dream of piloting the supersonic Buccaneer aircraft. This time, she told him that his latest ambition – to ride in the ultimate steeplechase, the Grand National – was 'out of the question'. And she urged him not to risk any injuries which might result in his hobbling down the aisle of St Paul's on the big day – or even in the wedding having to be postponed. Scarcely reassuring, in the circumstances, was the advice of Lord Oaksey, one of the top post-war amateur riders and now 'Marlborough' of the *Daily Telegraph*:

> I think the Prince should be allowed to do exactly what he pleases. He is quite likely to have another fall, but the risks are the same for anyone riding in a steeplechase. It is well known that this is a hazardous way of spending an afternoon. . . . Most of those injuries are ephemeral – bruising, breaking bones or at worst concussion. But people have been killed. I suppose on average there has been about one fatality every two years since the war.

The great royal steeplechase seemed, for the moment at least, to be over.

There is always the consolation of polo, his love of which the Prince has inherited from his father. He once captained the Young England team, but has since just failed to reach the very top standard. He doesn't practise enough, say his polo chums, to be the world-class player he should be; he doesn't spend enough (a mere £20,000 a year) on his string of ponies, to whom he is not brutal enough on the field of play. Not surprising, perhaps, for a man whom Berlioz's *L'Enfance du Christ* can still (at the x-thousandth hearing) reduce to tears. Shooting and fishing, reading (mostly history and biographies) and listening to his stereo complete the list. All rather solitary pursuits. But the Prince, as we have seen, has been leading a rather solitary life.

Until now. Lady Diana's arrival on the royal scene will bring a much-needed breath of air into Prince Charles's life at a time when his fortunes and his friendships have been standing forlornly still. Now to be the intimate of a man with few close friends, and with many secrets to share, she will also bring to his life the freshness of her generation – and, for all her own privileged background, some of the values of the outside world, which is often perceived but dimly from behind the lace-curtained windows of Buckingham Palace.

He is acknowledged, with his grandmother, to be the most soft-hearted and thoughtful member of his family, qualities he will certainly bring to his marriage as he has to their courtship. He now seeks above all to attempt to recreate for himself the happy family life he has seen his parents enjoy, and which has had such a profound influence on his character and upbringing. Not for him the stern paternalism of George V, father of Edward VIII and George VI: 'My father was frightened of his mother; I was frightened of my father, and I am damned well going to see to it that my children are frightened of me.'

The present Royal Family's good relations, by contrast, are very much a matter of mutual respect and affection between the generations. (As in most families, what arguments there are tend to be conducted sideways, rather than up and down, on the family tree.) Prince Charles has always looked on his grandmother, Queen Elizabeth, as a uniquely close confidante, an unfailing source of the kind of advice and reassurance which can often come more easily from grandparents than from parents. Now, as he had hoped, she is playing the same role for Diana. Although Diana moved out of Clarence House, to live with her sister Jane, a week after the engagement announcement, the Queen Mother continued to lay on for her what amounted to a master-class in conduct becoming a Princess and future Queen. There were some raised eyebrows and tsk-tsks, for instance, very soon after the engagement announcement, when Diana chose to escort her fiancé on their first public outing together in that dramatically décolleté evening gown; it set the nation (and the royal photographers) on a roar, but it distinctly failed to earn the QEQM Seal of Approval.

Charles's late great-uncle, Lord Mountbatten, played very much the same role in his life, after the premature death of his grandfather, King George VI. At Mountbatten's graveside, after weeping publicly at his funeral, Charles left a wreath inscribed simply: 'To HGF from HGS' – to Honorary Grandfather from Honorary Grandson. The Royal Family's elder statesman had been among the closest friends of three British monarchs this century, including the last Prince of Wales, the future Duke of Windsor, whose example he always urged Charles to study, but to shun. His death left an aching gap in Prince Charles's life which there was no one at all to fill.

In time, with luck on both sides, Prince Philip will take Mountbatten's place in Prince Charles's life. Relations between father and son have hitherto, on occasion, been volatile. It has not been easy for the Duke of Edinburgh, constantly living in his bride's shadow, constantly outranked by his eldest son in the family's order of precedence. It has not been easy for Charles, often dressed down rather harshly by a father whom he much respects, and who has set him a tough act to follow. At each of his schools, Charles had his father's shining example to live up to; he may have outstripped him in the academic stakes – and onstage, where Charles played Gordonstoun's Macbeth, Philip having merely been Donalbain – but he was always a lap or two behind on the more public sports field. The consolation for both is that Prince Philip recognizes what a pillar Mountbatten, his own uncle, had become in Prince Charles's life, and knows all too well how much his son will need the support of an older, more experienced figure.

There will be a poignant reminder on the wedding day of the esteem in which Elizabeth II holds her husband – when the Prince of Wales, like his sister before him, signs the register with the surname of Mountbatten-Windsor. Princes, in the normal course of things, just don't have surnames; Charles usually signs himself just plain Charles. But the Queen deliberately recognized Prince Philip's 'major contribution to British life' by an edict dated 8 February 1960, which decreed: 'It is my Will and Pleasure that, while I and my children shall continue to be styled and known as the House and Family of Windsor, my descendants . . . and their descendants shall bear the name of Mountbatten-Windsor.' There was something of a constitutional furore, the decree having been ambiguously worded, but it was resolved by the Lord Chancellor of the day, who overruled all the wrangling constitutional lawyers with the simple verdict: whatever the Queen says goes. What the Queen had said, in effect, was that she wished her husband's name to be linked with hers in the eyes of posterity.

Once the nuptial hullabaloo is over, and the nation slips back to normal, Charles and Diana will be permitted to slide quietly off into the greater privacy of country life at Highgrove, to start practising the homespun philosophy of marriage he has always preached:

> Whatever your place in life, when you marry you are forming a partnership which you hope will last fifty years. . . . Creating a secure family unit in which to bring up children, and give them a happy, secure upbringing – that's what marriage is all about. . . . I hope I will be as lucky as my parents, who have been so happy.

His younger brothers, most immediately Prince Andrew, will then begin to take over more of Charles's ritualistic public duties, to allow him the time to build his marriage and his family life. The Prince and Princess of Wales will also be within easy reach of Princess Anne's Gloucestershire home, his once somewhat strained relations with his sister having improved dramatically since the birth of her first child, his godson Peter Phillips. We are likely to see less of him in London.

Prince Andrew, meanwhile, for all the glamorous publicity he has already won himself, will be expected by his parents to earn a more solid public reputation. Charles's marriage is producing a conscious changing of the royal guard at the Palace, with Andrew being groomed to use the occasion for his emergence into a fuller public life. The Queen has not been altogether happy with his ill-disguised enjoyment of his princely position in his late teens and early twenties. When her children were young, she decreed that members of the Royal Household should call them by their Christian names until they reached the age of eighteen, when they were to be addressed as 'Sir'; significantly, on Prince Andrew's eighteenth birthday in 1978, the Queen instructed her staff that the rule need not yet be observed. Now that he has reached twenty-one, he is accorded his due eminence, but his mother still shudders whenever she hears him referred to as 'Randy Andy'. There is very much a sense, among Palace staff, that Andrew is now entering on a period of public probation.

He may quickly inherit his brother's discarded title of 'the world's most eligible bachelor', but it may be some time yet before he wins himself the kind of accolade bestowed on Prince Charles recently by one ecstatic hagiographer:

> ... the most accomplished young man in Britain ... rich, handsome, intelligent and eligible – the Twentieth Century Renaissance man, who has done everything, been everywhere, met everyone that matters ... he is actor, sportsman, pilot, musician, artist, orator, academic, wit, sailor and future King.

British women's magazines tend to get a bit carried away on grand royal occasions, but even HRH might acknowledge this as laying it on a bit thick. The celebration of his wedding is, however, an apt moment for the nation to acknowledge that he has proved himself a more unpretentious, well-intentioned and dedicated prince than a country has any right to expect of one born to be its Head of State – more so, to be sure, than many of his predecessors as Prince of Wales. Britain and the Commonwealth, in short, have been lucky. Or, as Lord Mountbatten put it shortly before his death: 'It's not luck at all. It's a bloody miracle.'

CHAPTER FOUR

The Thrill of the Chase

THE British press has been marrying off Prince Charles since he was three years old. In 1952, immediately after his mother's accession to the throne, the first of countless lists of eligible brides appeared in a Sunday newspaper, casting its net around all the European royal houses as well as the stately homes of England. Of the hundreds of candidates canvassed, concocted and chased over the next thirty years, not once – until the late summer of 1980 – was the name of Lady Diana Spencer mentioned. When the Prince of Wales said on 17 June 1977, the day the *Daily Express* announced his betrothal to Princess Marie-Astrid, 'I have not yet met the girl I want to marry', he was speaking the truth.

Sort of. Charles and Diana, as we have seen, have known each other all their lives, though to him she was always his younger brother's playmate. It has been said, predictably enough, that she has 'always' been in love with him ... that she has loved him since her eighth birthday, the day he was invested as Prince of Wales at Caernarvon ... that she has loved him since the summer of 1977, when the nation was convinced he was going to marry Marie-Astrid, while all the time he was wooing Diana's elder sister, Sarah.

They 'met', as they have now told the world, 'in a ploughed field' at Althorp in November 1977. Sarah had invited Charles to a shoot on her father's estate, and for the first time the world's most eligible bachelor, always somewhat gauche and ill-at-ease with the ladies, noticed that his girlfriend's younger sister was suddenly blossoming into a handsome and engaging young woman – in his own words, 'a very amusing and jolly – and attractive – sixteen-year-old'. For her part, as the world now knows, Diana thought her Prince had come. Charles was 'pretty amazing'.

The Prince once said of the subject of marriage: 'Well, it's the last decision on which I would want my head to be ruled by my heart.' Lady Diana was put on ice in the royal head and heart for the best part of three years, while the dashing bachelor sowed a few wild oats, being seen in the company of film stars, pop singers, English roses, elder sisters, younger sisters, even the odd divorcée. Then, in the summer of 1980, Diana came to stay at Balmoral, and stood patiently on the riverbank, immortal longings in her heart, as her Prince demonstrated his prowess at fly-fishing. It turned out she could catch the odd salmon, too.

By this time Sarah Spencer had fallen by the wayside. Red-haired, vivacious, an ideal public escort, Sarah had suffered from *anorexia nervosa*, 'the slimmer's disease', when they first noticed each other at Ascot in the summer of 1977. Charles had sympathetically helped her back to good health, and they were soon indulging their mutual love of outdoor sports. A ten-day skiing holiday with the Duke and Duchess of Gloucester in January 1978 led to press innuendo about the number of bedrooms in their Klosters villa, but Sarah insisted on her return that the relationship was platonic. In conversation with a women's magazine, she went further: 'I am not in love with him ... and I wouldn't marry anyone I didn't love, whether it was the dustman or the King of England. If he asked me, I would turn him down.'

Charles was more hurt than annoyed. Sarah had broken the golden rule of never, but never, talking to the press. But the Prince did not, contrary to public belief, 'drop' her immediately after the incident: Sarah was a guest of the Queen at Sandringham the following New Year. She herself, however, had noticed Charles's eye now straying to her younger sister. 'They just clicked,' said Sarah of the encounter in the ploughed field. 'He met Miss Right and she met Mr Right.' Sarah's claim to a footnote in history – now that she, like so many of Charles's other sometime girlfriends, had married someone else – was that she had brought them together: 'I played Cupid.'

Of that heady Balmoral summer, three years on, Charles now says: 'I began to realize what was going on in my mind, and hers in particular.' When he invited Diana back in September, after inundating her London flat with flowers, the press also began to realize what was going on. Thus began the hounding of 'Shy Di', one of the most extraordinary episodes in the turbulent history of royal relations with the press.

Unknown to anyone, the couple had been enjoying clandestine meetings that autumn at the Queen Mother's Scottish home, Birkhall. Fleet Street had lost the scent by November, when Diana was noticed to be a guest at Princess Margaret's birthday bash at the Ritz Hotel. She sat at dinner, one of the departing guests informed the waiting newshounds, next to Prince Charles. The approach of the Prince's birthday on 14 November – by now a traditional catalyst for tidal waves of marriage rumours – was all the excuse Fleet Street needed.

For the next ten days Diana was hounded from pillar to post, with cameramen disguising themselves as roadsweepers outside the Young England school, and even climbing in the lavatory window. If her car stalled, it was front-page news. There was a momentary distraction when a German magazine, *Die Aktuelle*, superimposed Princess Marie-Astrid's head on a photograph of an old Charles flame, Sabrina Guinness, walking with the Prince at Ascot; but she was soon to become engaged to a German count, Georg Von Und Zu Eltz, finally putting the kibosh on one of Fleet Street's most cherished myths. So all eyes were back on Lady Di, but the royal birthday came and went without a word, without even a clue. They didn't even spend the day together. Now the disappointment infected the 'quality' papers as well: 'The Court Circular that issued from Buckingham Palace last night', wrote the *Guardian*, 'was profoundly disappointing for a nation which, beset by economic and political dissent, had briefly believed that the sound of distant tumbrils was to be drowned by the peals of royal wedding bells.'

Battle was rejoined in earnest, with Prince Charles himself refuelling the fires by telling reporters freezing outside his Sandringham front door: 'Why don't you all go home to your wives? ... You'll all be told soon enough.' Told what? Speculation remounted. The following day, 16 November, the *Sunday Mirror* 'revealed exclusively' that the Prince and Lady Diana had enjoyed two late-night rendezvous on the royal train 'as it stood in a secluded sidings in Wiltshire'. Under cover of darkness, said the paper, Diana 'was ushered through a police road block to the waiting train' after 'a 100-mile dash by car from her home in London' on the nights of 5 and 6 November.

Elizabeth II was not amused. The story was immediately denied by

Buckingham Palace, but the Queen was so furious that she took the unprecedented step of ordering her press secretary, Michael Shea, to demand a retrac-
tion. He wrote to the editor of the *Sunday Mirror*, Robert Edwards, 'to protest
in the strongest possible terms about the totally false story', which was 'a total
fabrication'. Grave exception, he went on, had been taken in Palace circles
to 'the implication of the story', and an apology was demanded.

None was given. The following Sunday's *Mirror* printed Shea's letter in full
on the front page, together with Edwards's reply and a further letter from Shea.
The *Mirror*, said its editor, 'stood by' its story, and Shea was left 'to consider
what further action should be taken'. The Queen seriously considered taking
the newspaper to the Press Council, a move the Royal Family had made only
once before, when revealing photographs of Princess Margaret water-skiing
had been ruled 'an unwarranted intrusion' in 1964. In Prince Charles's childhood, the Queen had on several occasions had her private secretary circulate
Fleet Street editors with requests that reporters stop disrupting his school life at
Hill House, Cheam, and later at Gordonstoun. At one stage editors were
summoned to tea at Buckingham Palace and told that, unless they co-operated,
the Prince would be withdrawn from his school, and the great royal education
experiment ended, with the blame resting firmly on the British press. He was
left in peace for a while, but his Gordonstoun years were marred by a succession
of fabricated stories, climaxing in the theft of his exercise books from his desk
and the subsequent publication of his school essays in German and American
magazines.

The saga of the royal train – quickly dubbed 'Love in the Sidings' around
Fleet Street – was still bubbling on when the Press Association, on 27 November,
put out an interview with Lady Diana in which she was quoted as saying, 'I'd
like to marry soon.' Next day, publicly in tears, she denied ever having said it.
The PA, like the *Sunday Mirror*, stood by its story, but this time the Royal Family
made no move. Instead Diana's mother, her patience at an end, delivered
herself of her views in a terse letter to *The Times*:

> In recent weeks many articles have been labelled 'exclusive quotes', when the
> plain truth is that my daughter has not spoken the words attributed to her.
> Fanciful speculation, if it is in good taste, is one thing, but this can be
> embarrassing. Lies are quite another matter, and by their very nature, hurtful
> and inexcusable ...
>
> May I ask the editors of Fleet Street whether, in the execution of their jobs,
> they consider it necessary or fair to harass my daughter daily, from dawn until
> well after dusk? Is it fair to ask any human being, regardless of circumstances,
> to be treated in this way? The freedom of the press was granted by law, by

public demand, for very good reasons. But when these privileges are abused, can the press command any respect, or expect to be shown any respect?

Mrs Shand-Kydd, writing from her home on the Isle of Seil, pointed out that the decision to write the letter had been reached 'by me alone, and without consultation'. But there was little doubt of tacit endorsement from the Palace. By this time it had been decided there that resort to the Press Council might only make matters worse – despite Bob Edwards's dubious assertion that his story 'in no way reflected badly on Prince Charles or Lady Diana' – and the Press Council had meanwhile decided against launching an inquiry on its own initiative. But even the press itself began to wonder if things had gone too far. As sixty MPs tabled a motion in the House of Commons 'deploring the manner in which Lady Diana Spencer is treated by the media', and 'calling upon those responsible to have more concern for individual privacy', Fleet Street editors met senior Press Council members to discuss the issues involved. It was the first time in the Council's twenty-seven-year history that an extraordinary meeting of this kind had been convened. There was much criticism of the way the Palace was handling the romance rumours – memories still being fresh of firm denials from the Palace of an engagement between Princess Anne and Mark Phillips in 1973, a week before it was announced. There was also a consensus that poor Mr Shea himself did not know what was going on. The *Guardian* wrote:

> Seventy-five per cent of the speculation would die away if the Palace would quietly explain the situation. Alas, there is no attempt at explanation. ... Rather, one finds a growing feeling that somehow Lady Diana is being tested. ... It would be pleasant to see tabloid editors forsake the kindergarten; but that – in the real world – would be far more easily accomplished if the Palace plumped for open government, rather than cat-and-mouse silences.

In the end, amid a certain amount of righteous indignation, Fleet Street decided to cool it.

Not for long. On 15 December the *Guardian*, of all papers, revealed exclusively that the engagement of Prince Charles and Lady Diana would be announced 'today'. The craving for 'exclusive' engagement announcements had spread even to the 'quality' papers. The reason for this sudden abandonment of the Fleet Street pact, however, was a 'summit meeting' (*Sun, Star, Daily Mirror*) at Sandringham that weekend between the Royal Family and members of the Spencer family. This, at last, must be it. The Queen would surely take the opportunity of her televised Christmas Day message to the nation to pass on the happy news.

It wasn't, and she didn't.

As the Battle of Sandringham was joined over the New Year, with the Queen shouting angrily at the press for the first time in her life, the tabloid indignation reached fever point. The *Daily Mirror* thundered:

> The editors of Fleet Street won't mind Prince Charles wishing them a Nasty New Year. They are fair game. But when the teenage Prince Edward fires a gun 20 yards from a photographer on a public road, he should be told to cool it . . .
>
> Buckingham Palace would not say whether Lady Diana was going to Sandringham. If they had said she wasn't going, the press would have drifted away. If they had said she was going, the press would have been there that day. Saying nothing meant they got the press every day . . .
>
> If Lady Diana Spencer is to be the future Queen of England, she cannot expect to be Greta Garbo as well.

On 8 January Charles and Diana enjoyed a dawn rendezvous on the Berkshire Downs, at the Lambourn stables of his trainer Nick Gaselee. The newshounds caught up with them a couple of hours later, in time to take photographs of their two empty cars standing poignantly nose-to-nose. (In the *Daily Mirror* soon after, one columnist perhaps overestimated Lady Diana's skills behind the wheel of her Mini Metro, when lodging an indignant complaint that Prince Charles expected her to drive 'more than 150 miles' to see him: 'She had to get there by 7 am,' he explained, 'which meant a 6 am start from London.')

It was to be the last time any of their secret rendezvous were rumbled – despite several more meetings at Highgrove, and at the nearby home of the Parker-Bowleses – before Charles departed on his annual skiing holiday to Klosters, as the guests of his friends Charles and Patti Palmer-Tomkinson. He took the Duke and Duchess of Gloucester for company, and most of the British press in his slipstream. But the original plan that Diana should go too was abandoned, ostensibly because she 'wanted him to be left in peace for a while'; so soon before the announcement of their engagement, however, a shared vacation would have overstepped the bounds of royal propriety.

There was soon an occasion for indignation all round, when the German magazine *7 Days* published a mock-up cover photo of Charles looking on proudly as Diana cradled an infant, saying, 'I want to give the Prince many pretty babies.' Shocking, said Fleet Street, while the Prince merely shrugged in despair on the ski slopes, and back in London Lady Diana again dissolved into public tears.

It was, at the last, the ultimate quality newspaper, *The Times* itself, which broke the news of the engagement on the morning it was to be announced. It

From the family album: Diana's parents marry at Westminster Abbey in 1954; their third daughter is christened seven years later; and enjoys a family outing to the zoo (astride camel).

Althorp, the Spencer family seat since the sixteenth century. Diana's young brother, Charles, Viscount Althorp, shows weekend visitors the family heirlooms.

Diana *(right)* is a bridesmaid at her sister Jane's wedding in 1978. Her father and his new wife, Raine Dartmouth, open a shop in their stately home. The former Countess Spencer, now Mrs Peter Shand-Kydd, arrives home from Australia to congratulate her daughter – and future Queen.

A Prince is born: the *News Chronicle* announces the news; Cecil Beaton takes the first portrait. Before the arrival of Andrew and Edward, the Royal Family enjoys a Balmoral summer.

A happy, relaxed interlude with the Mountbattens in Malta . . . and just another
undergraduate in the Trinity College freshmen's photo.

Leaders of fashion?: the last Prince of Wales, the future King Edward VIII and Duke of Windsor, in a snappy jersey; his successor in a safer grey suit. And a comparative study in toppers.

The world's most eligible bachelor: the Prince of Wales meets Farrah Fawcett . . . and dallies, amid the polo ponies, with Lady Jane Wellesley and Lady Sarah Spencer, elder sister of his future bride.

On duty in India (in yet another royal hat); off duty at Sandringham and at Klosters.

Pursuit by paparazzi: Diana at bay as the uncertainty mounts.

Fleeing . . . but where? Diana climbs into her famous Mini Metro . . . then stalls it.

Time to reflect: Charles hunts in Cheshire, Diana strolls round her family's estate at Althorp.

Minds have been made up: Charles and Diana, both smiling, leave Lambourn after their dawn rendezvous.

It's official at last: Diana's father and stepmother join the crowd outside Buckingham Palace;
the happy couple dine that evening with their grandmothers; and Inspector Paul Officer
keeps a watchful eye on his master's bride-to-be.

In the paddock at Sandown: Diana makes her first appearance with other royals, and shows she too can wear a hat . . .

Disaster at Sandown: the Prince of
Wales takes a tumble, and hangs his
head in shame.

The dress that stunned the world: Diana takes a firm hold of her reputation . . . and meets Princess Grace of Monaco.

was an appropriate scoop for the proud new owner of *The Times*, Mr Rupert Murdoch, to savour in the first week of his proprietorship. It was also a blow to the bloodied but unbowed 'Charles-watchers'. Journalists who had spent the better part of their adult lives in pursuit of this moment had finally to concede defeat to the one newspaper which had all along remained aloof from the fray. But how had it happened?

Fleet Street's resentful finger was pointed immediately in the direction of Mr Edward Heath, the former Conservative Prime Minister, who was known to have lunched with the then editor of *The Times*, William Rees-Mogg, the day before. Mr Heath denied vehemently that he was the source of the leak. But it was known that the paper had acted on a tip from 'someone very important' to Mr Rees-Mogg, who had been observed to rush into the office late that evening and dictate the story to a reporter in time to make the second edition. Where had he been to dinner? Furious enquiries were made, but to no avail.

The truth of the matter is that Mr Rees-Mogg dined alone, at home, in Smith Square. He had indeed lunched with Mr Heath that day, but insists that it was not Heath who tipped him off. 'It was a purely private lunch, and the matter did not come up.' Someone – whose identity Mr Rees-Mogg intends to take with him to his grave – telephoned the editor of *The Times* at his home that evening, to tell him that the engagement would be announced at 11 am the next morning.

Although it is still thought that only about a dozen people knew in advance of the timing of the announcement, a truer estimate would be something over two hundred. The Prime Minister, as she herself said, had felt obliged to inform certain of her Cabinet ministers; members of the Royal Family and the Spencer family were excitedly passing the news – in the strictest confidence, of course – one to the other. Strong hints had already been dropped, through diplomatic channels, into the private offices of those world leaders who would have to fit the wedding into their schedules. That Monday, Buckingham Palace realized that the whole thing was getting out of hand. Their cherished plan to take Fleet Street by surprise, after all the strained relations of the previous few weeks, were suddenly in danger. There was brief consideration of bringing the announcement forward to Monday evening; but that was overtaken by the news of the attempted coup in Spain, which was preoccupying not only Fleet Street but certain members of the Royal Family (King Juan Carlos is a close friend of the Prince of Wales).

So Buckingham Palace was scooped by *The Times*. Prince Charles was distinctly annoyed. But the rest of the day went well: Diana handled their various joint interviews with great aplomb, and was tactful enough to stand on the step below her Prince for the engagement photographs, so as to avoid towering over him as the pictures went round the world. And the rest of the week saw the predictable explosion of royal hysteria, front pages cooing 'So In Love' and 'My Shy Di' to herald interminable special supplements. The thrill of the chase was dead; long live happily-ever-after. Exit the investigative teams; enter the saccharine squad. Apart from the happy couple themselves, no one was more relieved to see the end of the royal siege than the Queen's long-suffering press secretary, Michael Shea.

Never had a Prince of Wales been compelled to conduct so public a romance. Previous Princes had suffered the most vicious lampooning (such as the Prince Regent experienced at the hands of Rowlandson) and a sycophancy even more undiluted than that served up today (such as greeted the engagement of the future Edward VII to Princess Alexandra of Denmark in 1863). But Prince Charles has never in his life been able to enjoy the freedom of movement available even to the last Prince of Wales, the future King Edward VIII and Duke of Windsor, who later recalled in his memoirs 'with wonder and appreciation the ease with which we were able to move about in public places'. The ensuing paragraph, written with the elegance which characterizes *A King's Story* (1951), must enhance Prince Charles's occasional yearnings to have been born in a previous age:

> The thought occurs to me that one of the most inconvenient developments since the days of my boyhood has been the disappearance of privacy. I grew up before the age of the flash camera, when newspapers still employed large staffs of artists to depict the daily events with pen sketches. This artistic form of illustration seldom achieved the harsh or cruel accuracy of the camera lens, nor would it match the volume and mobility of the present-day photographer dogging his unsuspecting victim or waiting for a candid shot. Because our likenesses seldom appeared in the press, we were not often recognized on the street; when we were, the salutation would be a friendly wave of the hand or, in the case of a courtier or family friend, a polite lifting of the hat.

Even as that passage was being written, two-year-old Prince Charles's nannies were being obliged to abandon their walks around St James's Park because of the attentions of photographers and sightseers, and Prince Philip was delivering himself of his immortal verdict on the ladies and gentlemen of the Fourth Estate: 'God save us from those bloody vultures.' Lady Diana was herself only two years old when the *Weekly Tribune* of Geneva wrote of her future husband's Bavarian skiing holiday in 1963: 'It was like a snow scene from a Keystone cops movie, as impatient voices bawled suggestions in English, French, Italian and

German, their cars revving madly, wheels spinning, as they leaped, slithered and bumped into each other in a frantic race for the best positions behind the speeding sleighs.' Now, two decades later, she had herself survived the ultimate 'ordeal by vulture' – which her future parents-in-law did indeed regard to some extent, as the *Guardian* suspected, as a prerequisite for their approval of the match. In another of her testy New Year asides at Sandringham, the Queen was overheard to declare: 'Well, she's going to have to learn to get used to this sort of thing. At least it's useful in that respect.'

In Prince Charles's case, it was not just his final romance but his entire discovery of the subject – and subsequently enthusiastic exploration of it – which was considered fair game by the contemporary mass media. Given that he is a self-confessed romantic – a man, by his own account, 'who falls in love easily' and has done so 'on countless occasions' – there has been plenty for the popular press to chronicle. Apart from the respectful lists of eligible European princesses submitted throughout his childhood, the ever lengthening litany of his flames, companions, escorts and true loves has been trotted out with monotonous regularity now for something over ten years. Ever since Lucia Santa Cruz, daughter of the then Chilean ambassador to London, captured his youthful heart at Cambridge, there have been at least two or three names a year for the British public to conjure with. From the Cambridge days of Lucia, Sybilla Dorman (daughter of the then Governor-General of Malta) and the Buxton girls (daughters of Prince Philip's naturalist friend, Aubrey Buxton), the line stretches through the Seventies to his sprees with Sabrina Guinness, Jane Ward and Anna Wallace in the twelve months before the summer of Balmoral, the riverbank and Diana.

The roll-call from my previous book, *Charles, Prince of Wales* (described in his review by Enoch Powell MP as 'distasteful', but reprinted here – in updated form – in the interests of combining comprehensiveness with brevity) included:

Lady Leonora Grosvenor, daughter of the Duke of Westminster (now married to the Earl of Lichfield, better known as Patrick Lichfield, the photographer); her sister *Lady Jane Grosvenor*, now the Duchess of Roxburghe; *Lady Victoria Percy*, daughter of the Duke of Northumberland, a Roman Catholic, now married to John Cuthbert, a wealthy landowner; her sister *Lady Caroline Percy*, now married to the Spanish Count Pierre de Cabarrus; *Bettina Lindsay*, daughter of the Conservative politician Lord Balniel, now Mrs Peter Drummond-Hay; *Lady Cecil Kerr*, daughter of the Marquess of Lothian, now married to Donald Cameron of Lochiel; *Lady Henrietta Fitzroy*, daughter of the Duke of Grafton, now married to a fifty-year-old lawyer named Edward St George (who had been previously married to Kathleen, daughter of the bookie's bookie, William Hill); *Lady Charlotte Manners*, daughter of the Duke of Rutland; her cousin *Elizabeth 'Libby' Manners*; *Angela Nevill*, daughter of Prince Philip's private secretary, Lord Rupert Nevill; *Lady Camilla Fane*, daughter of the Earl of Westmorland; *Caroline Longman*, daughter of the wealthy publisher, the late Mark Longman; Lord Astor of Hever's daughter *Louise Astor*, who married David Herring, brother of Prince Charles's recent friend, Mrs Jane Ward; *Georgiana Russell*, daughter of the diplomat Sir John Russell, now Mrs Brooke Boothby; and *Rosie Clifton*, the colonel's daughter, now married to the Prince of Wales's polo-playing chum Mark Vestey.

The catalogue could go on and on, though readers should bear in mind Charles's own heartfelt words to his attendant journalists while in India last year: 'It's all right for you chaps. You can live with a girl before you marry her. But I can't. I've got to get it right from the word go.' But three other names deserve especial pride of place in any chronicle of the Prince's romantic past: Lady Sarah Spencer, Diana's elder sister, Davina Sheffield and Lady Jane Wellesley.

Charles met Lady Sarah on the rebound from Davina, the soldier's daughter, ex-debutante, blonde, dramatically attractive, one of the few girlfriends with whom he has been so publicly carried away as to allow himself to be photographed arm-in-arm with her. He met her at a time of tragedy, in 1976, when she was brought home from refugee work in Vietnam by the brutal murder of her mother by raiders in their Oxfordshire home. Of all the Prince's girlfriends who have fallen foul of the artificial code by which he must live, and be seen to live, Davina was the one whose loss he felt most dearly. Not for the first or the last time, it was a jealous ex-boyfriend who put paid to the relationship by letting on to a London gossip columnist that he and Davina had once lived together. Charles could never be romantically linked with her again. (A similar fate befell a more passing fancy, the voluptuous Fiona Watson, daughter of the Yorkshire landowner Lord Manton, when another embittered ex-beau helped Fleet Street unearth – and revel in – the fact that she had once displayed her startling 38–23–35 assets in full colour across eleven pages of *Penthouse* magazine.)

Lady Jane Wellesley, an enduring friend since childhood, was long the bookies' favourite, and certainly showed most staying power in a highly competitive field. The daughter of the Duke of Wellington, Jane had all the obvious characteristics: an impeccable aristocratic pedigree, and a handsome English rose exterior behind which ticked a brain worthy of the most intelligent heir to the throne for many a year. Before Diana entered Prince Charles's life, Jane was perhaps the girl he came closest to marrying; and she was certainly Diana's most conspicuous predecessor as a victim of siege by Fleet Street. Through much of 1973 and 1974, she was compelled to pick her way to work at the BBC through an army of photographers and writers in permanent camp on her Chelsea doorstep. In early 1973, during a holiday at her father's ancestral estate in Spain, reporters watched breathlessly through high-powered binoculars as she pulled the Prince of Wales's hair and 'playfully threw melons at him'. Many a statement was issued denying anything more than friendship, but Jane's appearance at Sandringham later that year as a weekend guest of the Queen was enough to draw a crowd of 10,000 to the scene (at a time of acute petrol shortage). She has always denied that she turned the Prince down, despite constant suggestions that she was one of the few unprepared to contemplate so irrevocable a surrender of her freedom. But the truth is that Prince Charles was about to enter on his career in the Services, and knew that much of the next six years would be spent travelling away from home. Unlike many a Prince of Wales before him, he was unwilling to leave behind a young wife pining, Penelope-like, for his return.

Jane remains a lasting friend, still pursuing a busy career in television, where she is now researching a documentary on the Spanish Civil War for an independent network. But even when her age, as she approached thirty, ruled her out of consideration, certain quarters of Fleet Street could not bring themselves to accept her withdrawal from the interminable royal marriage stakes. As recently as 1979, when she arranged a photo session for Claire Bloom in her role as public relations officer for the BBC Shakespeare plays, it was Jane whose photograph appeared in the next day's papers. When, in the same capacity, she paid a routine visit to the television editor of the *Sun* newspaper, photographers intent on updating their files were hanging from the rafters.

Many of Prince Charles's old flames (with the notable exception of Lady Jane) are now married, and some will be admitted to the inner circle of royal friends, the makings of the 'junior court' over which Charles and Diana will in time preside. Few, however, are likely to take the place in his affections of the two married women to whom he is especially close: Dale Tryon and Camilla Parker-Bowles. Like his great-uncle the Duke of Windsor, when he was Prince of Wales, Charles has found a unique security in the close friendship of married women. He could be seen with them, for one thing, without any danger of starting more wearisome marriage rumours. They are able, for another, to offer him much-needed comfort and advice, without either party having to worry about declarations of interest. Charles is godfather to both their eldest children.

Australian-born Dale, now thirty-one, whom the Prince affectionately calls

'Kanga', is the wife of Lord (Anthony) Tryon, forty-one-year-old son of the Queen's late treasurer, a director of Lazard Brothers, the merchant bankers, and chairman of the finance firm English and Scottish Investors Ltd. Among the few fixed points on Charles's annual schedule are his summer fishing trip with the Tryons to their secluded lodge near Egilsstadir, in Iceland, and regular weekends – in season, for the pheasant shooting – on their 700-acre estate in Wiltshire. Charles first met 'Kanga' in Australia at a teenage hop organized by Timbertops, the 'outback annexe' of the Geelong school he attended in 1966. They spent most of the evening together, and he sought her out every time he returned to Australia – until she married Lord Tryon in 1975, and made her home at the Tryon family seat in Wiltshire.

Across the border in Gloucestershire, the Prince and Princess of Wales will also be neighbours of his other great friends, Camilla and Andrew Parker-Bowles, who are often separated by his career as a rising officer in the Household Cavalry. Andrew, now forty-one, was once a suitor to Princess Anne; he was promoted Lieutenant-Colonel (commanding the Knightsbridge barracks) after his term as an aide to Lord Soames during the negotiation of the independence of Rhodesia-Zimbabwe. In the course of his duties there he was required to 'try out' a buffalo for the Prince of Wales, before his arrival to preside at the independence ceremonies; for his pains, Parker-Bowles was gored, suffering on the Prince's behalf a wound which required twelve stitches. His wife Camilla is a niece of the Cubitt's building family millionaire, Lord Ashcombe.

Poor Diana, who faced stern enough tests on other fronts in her candidacy for the Prince's hand, had above all to pass the daunting 'acceptability test' imposed by Prince Charles in the winning of Dale Tryon's and Camilla Parker-Bowles's approval. Several before her had failed, notably Anna Wallace, the glamorous and outspoken 'ice maiden' who briefly dazzled the Prince – it is reliably believed that he asked her to marry him – before flouncing off to marry Johnny Hesketh, younger brother of the Lord Hesketh well-known for his involvement in Grand Prix motor racing. It was Anna who, Lily Langtry-like, publicly rebuked the Prince of Wales for ignoring her at the Queen Mother's eightieth birthday ball last year. As far as such breaches of royal protocol are concerned, little has changed in the last hundred or so years. Much though he may have deserved it – Prince Charles's behaviour towards discarded girlfriends has often been less than chivalrous – it sealed her fate with Dale and Camilla, whose hold over the Prince's powers of independent decision-making has of late become considerable. Anna Wallace, to be sure, was no longer acceptable at court.

It was, for instance, on their advice that Charles refused to return Sabrina

Guinness's telephone calls, or reply to her letters, once his affections had moved on – despite the fact that a royal marriage into 'the Irish beerage' was always out of the question. It was Dale and Camilla who headed up the committee of close friends which at a late stage compiled a list of 'acceptable' brides for the Prince, on which Lady Diana's name came out top. It is tempting to believe, on all the evidence, that only an innocent nineteen-year-old, much less worldly-wise than this daunting 'dynamic duo', could have met with their approval as supreme rival for the Prince's time and attention.

And so it came to pass, just before Christmas, that it was behind the Parker-Bowleses' Gloucestershire farmhouse, standing in the cabbage patch, that Prince Charles first raised the subject of marriage with Lady Diana Spencer. It was not, as yet, a formal proposal – more an '*If* I were to ask you, do you think it might be possible?' – but it amounted to a commitment, sanctioned in advance by his hostess and her husband. Diana, she has told friends, 'just giggled'. But her answer was never in doubt, for all the Prince's fears that the continued attentions of Europe's paparazzi might prematurely dull the enthusiasm of this young creature who had begun to captivate him, and whom he knew he could grow to love. If he were to lose her, he would not know where to turn for another so entirely suitable – so perfect for him, and so acceptable to his Queen and country.

A few months later, on the morning they announced their engagement, they were asked if they were in love. 'Of course,' said Diana, promptly and sensibly. 'Whatever "in love" means,' said Charles, rather more obscurely. And what of the age gap? 'I've never really thought about it,' said Diana, while con-ceding, 'I always ganged up with Prince Andrew.' Said her husband-to-be: 'You're only as young as you think you are. Diana will certainly keep me young.'

Next day, the Royal Family's latest recruit took to her new role as to the manner born, offering the crowds around Clarence House a practised royal wave within twenty-four hours of the announcement of her betrothal. She seemed likely, once she was put on, to prove most royally.

Having seen out six months of national speculation, however, she must prepare for another sustained bout as soon as she returns from her honeymoon. It was in May 1948, less than six months after her wedding to Prince Philip of Greece and Denmark, that the rumours began about Princess Elizabeth. On a visit to Paris she seemed, according to the French newspapers, 'tired and listless' in church. At a British Embassy reception in her honour that evening, she had met only half the guests when her husband led her from the room to rest. On 4 June, the eve of Derby Day, a Buckingham Palace statement announced simply that 'Her Royal Highness Princess Elizabeth, Duchess of Edinburgh, will undertake no public engagements after the end of June'.

Elizabeth gave the nation – and her husband – what they wanted, a male heir in direct line of succession to the throne, six days before her first wedding anniversary. In quite as short a time, England will expect Lady Di to be expecting.

CHAPTER FIVE

Send Them Victorious

AFTER their wedding, and the prolonged public scrutiny which attends it, the Prince and Princess of Wales will seek leave to absent themselves from publicity awhile. It will be granted. For the first time in as long as he can remember, Prince Charles will be able to disappear behind closed doors and begin to build himself some kind of private life. His Princess, for her part, will be able to ease herself gently into her brave, if daunting, new world.

The new Princess of Wales, the first in the lifetime of all but septuagenarian Britons, will find that her friends must drop her curtseys and call her 'Ma'am'. She will be required to escort her husband on divers public occasions, and will soon begin to undertake official engagements in her own right. As Prince Charles himself has pointed out, he 'began to do that kind of thing' at the age she is now: he was invested as Prince of Wales at Caernarvon at twenty, the age at which Lady Diana is marrying him.

She must grow accustomed to being a public icon, a piece of public property with only limited control over what is said, written or, to some degree, done about her. She must become used to seeing her face not merely on the kind of tea towels her mother refuses to stock in her Oban village store, but on postage stamps, biscuit tins, television screens, commemorative mugs, magazine covers, T-shirts – and perhaps one day, if she is lucky, money. She is already growing immune to something she must learn to accept utterly without complaint: reading acres of complete rubbish about herself and her family life in some of the public prints. She must develop an eye for the reporter disguised as a meter-reader, the photographer hidden in the gooseberry bush. Never again will she be allowed to use a bathroom on the ground floor of a public building.

These are but some of the more eccentric, less predictable, repercussions of 'becoming royal' Diana must learn to endure. But for the first few months, perhaps years, of her new life the Princess will be able to enjoy a good measure of the privacy so unfamiliar to her husband, and to the other central figures in the passing royal parade. As some of the more imaginative royal commentators chronicle her life in detail beyond anything they can possibly know, she will be able to live the real thing much as she chooses – especially in the nursery wing, which will be the focus of so much breathless anticipation. The several, quick-succession pregnancies expected of her will be excuse enough to stay out of the public eye for a while. If at first she doesn't want to, if she finds her wedding gives her a taste for public attention and adulation, she'll soon learn that there is plenty more where that came from. With a lifetime in the spotlight ahead, it would be wise to linger as long as possible in the wings.

Diana's new parents-in-law, the then Duke and Duchess of Edinburgh, had only just settled into their newly renovated London home, Clarence House, when fate dictated an early end to the years of tranquil domestic privacy for which they had hoped. It was on 4 July 1949 – as Prince Philip aptly pointed out, 'Independence Day', that the young couple and their nine-month-old baby Prince moved into Clarence House, where Princess Anne was born the following summer. It was a year of royal indulgences for all: Philip was spared much of his naval duty, and the Princess many of her public engagements, to spend as much time as they could with their young family. Nurses would wheel the children round St James's Park, at first without fear of recognition, and some-times up the road to Marlborough House, for a visit with their great-grand-mother ('Gan-Gan'), Queen Mary. Early in 1952, however, the King's health again began to fail, and Elizabeth and Philip had to undertake on his behalf an extensive Commonwealth tour. It was while they were away – Elizabeth was watching game from a Kenyan hunting-lodge called Treetops – that they learnt of George VI's death. The Prime Minister (Churchill), the Leader of the Opposition (Clement Attlee) and several members of the Cabinet were waiting with the late King's brother, the Duke of Gloucester, to welcome the young new Queen back to London the following day. It was an abrupt and much mourned end to life at Clarence House, and to family life as the young Royals had known it.

Queen Elizabeth II has herself spoken of 'the uncertainty of human life', but Charles and Diana should be spared such a fate for many years yet. Their children will most likely be adults, and they themselves grandparents, before they move into Buckingham Palace in their own right – which, by that time, they will be more than ready to do. Charles has spent the last twenty-eight years of his life living there, in a none too grand, rather chintzy suite of rooms which will now be inherited by one of his younger brothers. (Princess Anne retained her Palace suite after her marriage, but the heir to the throne will need a somewhat grander London residence.) The Prince will, however, maintain his suite of offices in the south-east corner of the main Palace courtyard, and will thus need a London home within easy striking distance.

For now, the Prince and Princess of Wales will be allocated a refurnished apartment in Kensington Palace, the royal 'condominium' which already houses Princess Margaret, Prince and Princess Michael of Kent and the Duke and Duchess of Gloucester. In time they will inherit Clarence House, Charles's first home, and Diana's temporary home in the first few days after her engagement. The fact is mentioned *sotto voce* in – even publicly denied by – Buckingham Palace, as it presupposes the death of the residence's very popular current occupant, Queen Elizabeth The Queen Mother. In the tradition of Queen Mary, however, Queen Elizabeth has become the revered matriarch of the British Royal Family, a symbol of continuity as much as of duty, and she is only too happy to know that her home will one day pass to the future King and Queen.

In the meantime Charles and Diana will begin their family life at Highgrove, the 350-acre country estate in Gloucestershire purchased by the Prince in 1980, for little less than a million pounds, from Maurice Macmillan MP, the son of the former Prime Minister. The listed Georgian house, near the South Cotswolds village of Tetbury, is only ten miles from the Gatcombe Park estate of Princess Anne and Captain Mark Phillips. Their Kent cousins will also be neighbours in what Prince Charles and his friends now call 'The Loyal Triangle'; Prince Michael recently acquired Lypiatt Manor, a period property near Stroud. Equally important, Highgrove is a mere ninety miles up the M4 motorway from central London, and thus just an hour's drive – if you stick to the speed limits – from Windsor and Heathrow Airport. It is also within easy striking distance of the Prince's Duchy of Cornwall estates around the West Country, to which he likes to pay frequent visits (and which financed the purchase of Highgrove).

The Waleses' new home has nine bedrooms (five with dressing-rooms *en suite*), six bathrooms, four spacious reception rooms, a nursery wing and a stable block, set in a 347-acre timbered estate which includes farmland and a dairy unit. It was first spotted by Princess Anne when she was house-hunting in the area; she ended up buying Gatcombe (from another Conservative politician, Lord Butler) and passed Highgrove on to her brother. When he visited it last year with the man from Humberts, the upper-crust estate agents, the Prince was immediately intrigued. After strolling around the impressive drawing-room, with its Irish marble fireplace and dolphin embellishments (the dolphin is the local motif), on through the library, the billiards room, the butler's pantry, kitchen and staff quarters, he took less than an hour to make up his mind while inspecting the immaculately maintained grounds. Lady Diana has since visited Highgrove with him many times, and is now supervising its redecoration, with the assistance of the Royal Family's favourite interior designer, Lord Mountbatten's son-in-law David Hicks. For the first few months after their wedding they will still be, as Charles put it, 'camping out'.

Another highly companionable, if less blue-blooded, neighbour will be the *Sunday Times* columnist Godfrey Smith, who recently advised the young Royals of some of the local amenities:

> ... Now for the food. I recommend the farmhouse cheddar at Jesse Smith's in Tetbury and the home-made brown bread and gentleman's relish at Country Provisions. Vacuum cleaners, electric kettles and washing machines may be entrusted for speedy repair to the Vac and Kettle Centre in Cirencester, while lobster and scallops fit for a princely tum may be had there at Charles Barnett. Health-giving brown rice and Muesli can be bought at the Great Western Whole Food shop there; fresh trout at the Alderley Trout Farm, and there's William's Kitchen at Nailsworth, a miniature Harrods food hall. Simplest of all, though, for the sporty girl would be to get a trolley and push it briskly round the Cirencester Waitrose, thus polishing off all the week's shopping in one energetic swoop.

Smith had already, as he put it, 'marked HRH's card' about the local beer, available at a healthy number of local hostelries – including one, just down the road from Highgrove, in the hamlet of Doughton, called The Prince of Wales. He also, however, reported 'a discordant note' among the locals: there had been 'mutterings from mean-spirited churls that the noticeable increase in police activity is bound to be reflected by a rise in the rates. Fortunately we still have two strong cells in the gates of Malmesbury Abbey, into which these curmud-geonly varlets can be thrown.'

E'en as Godfrey Smith was offering his own loyal welcome, the Tetbury town council voted unanimously to offer their distinguished new residents as a wedding present a handsome pair of wrought-iron gates for Highgrove. This despite mutterings 'from other curmudgeonly varlets that the ten-foot wall Prince Charles was erecting around the property was 'an eyesore'; reports in the Sunday press that extra security would be costing local councils anything up to £100,000 a year; and even one rather forward suggestion that Highgrove would be merely a temporary residence, and that the Prince of Wales really had his eye on nearby Badminton, at present occupied by the eighty-one-year-old Duke of Beaufort. Telephoned about the matter, the Duke spluttered appropriately angry denials.

The Duke is, of course, the Queen's host each year for the Badminton horse trials – and Highgrove is right in the heart of Beaufort Hunt country, which will suit the Prince (if not his bride); it is also handy for the Cheltenham races and polo at Cirencester. It is thus in every respect a happier choice for Prince Charles than was his previous country house, Chevening, with which he had a long and unfortunate love-hate relationship.

Chevening House, near Sevenoaks, in Kent, was bequeathed to the Prince of Wales by the seventh Earl Stanhope on his death in 1967. Set in its own 3,000-acre estate, with its own four-acre lake, the magnificent seventeenth-century mansion is in part attributed to Inigo Jones. Its Palladian Splendours, with two pavilions, colonnaded walkways, and thirty-six reception and state rooms, far outrank those of both Chequers and Dorneywood, the official country residences of the Prime Minister and the Foreign Secretary. Charles at first turned it down, after inspecting it with the Queen in 1969, when it was in need of extensive renovation. Five years later, however, after one wing had been briefly occupied by the Lord Chancellor, Lord Hailsham, he changed his mind, and a £250,000 rebuilding programme (financed by the Stanhope bequest) got under way. The Prince paid occasional visits of inspection – after discovering that the velvet lawns of Chevening were a mere twelve helicopter-minutes from Buckingham Palace – but his heart was never really in it. Local people were disappointed, even angry, that he sub-let the shooting rights and was so rarely there. They had envisaged Chevening as the centre of a glittering junior court, with galactical weekend parties worthy of the days of Bertie, Prince of Wales, a hundred years before. It came as no surprise when, on discovering Highgrove last summer, Charles finally renounced his rights to Chevening, which will now revert to the Government.

The Prince and Princess will also, of course, have suites of their own in each of the royal residences at which the Queen spends parts of each year: Windsor, Balmoral and Sandringham. They will be welcome at Holyrood House in Edinburgh, another home occasionally used by the sovereign, and will eventually inherit at least one of the castles already owned by the Royal Family in Scotland. But the Prince has so far, to the disappointment of his subjects in the principality of Wales, turned aside all offers of a Welsh residence. With perhaps another thirty years stretching ahead of him as Prince of Wales, and his record so far as a Prince who takes a dutiful interest in the country, this is a decision he may care to reconsider (especially if he proceeds with his plans to buy a house in Australia).

Another bonus will be a holiday cottage on the Scilly island of St Mary's: a tranquil three-bedroomed retreat, set behind high walls in its own half-acre, named Tamarisk after a locally luxuriant shrub. Among their neighbours here is Sir Harold Wilson, the former Prime Minister. Tamarisk, a few hundred yards from the local football pitch, convenient for helicopter landings, is part of the Prince's inheritance in his other primary role: Duke of Cornwall.

The heir to the throne is not, as is popularly supposed, automatically Prince of Wales; that is a title bestowed at the discretion of the sovereign. (Prince Charles was named Prince of Wales by his mother in 1958, at the age of nine, though he was not formally invested for another eleven years.) The heir to the throne *is*, however, *ex officio* Duke of Cornwall, Charles being the twenty-fourth since the Duchy's creation in 1337, when King Edward II bestowed it on the Black Prince. Since Prince Albert reformed its ancient and creaky machinery for his own son and heir, Bertie, the Duchy has become an extremely wealthy and profitable landowning enterprise, which will provide the Prince and Princess of Wales with the bulk of their income until Charles inherits the throne.

The great benefit to Charles and Diana of the Duchy's income is that it will keep them out of the annual rows in Parliament over the Civil List, the public money voted each year to cover some of the Royal Family's running expenses. The Civil List debate is always an excuse for the vociferous republican minority, led by Willie Hamilton MP, to sound off about the 'cost' of the monarchy, yet the amount awarded (£3.96 million in 1981) is but a pittance compared to the amount of 'invisible' revenue generated by the Royal Family in terms of tourism, souvenirs and other such British industries which would not be the same without them.

Even now, there is widespread public misunderstanding about the function of the Civil List. 'Queen Gets 12 Per Cent' and 'Royals Beat Pay Freeze' yelled opportunist headlines in the tabloid press after the March 1981 Budget. But as *The Times* rightly pointed out:

> An increase does not represent an increase in the personal incomes of the Queen and the members of her family who are on [the Civil List].... What it really represents is an increase in the costs of performing the public duties of Head of State and the associated duties of members of the Royal Family. Other people's wages take most of it.

Treasury officials are discussing the new Princess's source of income with the Palace, but it is unlikely that they will add to the Royal Family's periodic embarrassments by seeking to assign her a share of the Civil List fund. In principle, the 1972 Civil List Act made provision for the Princess of Wales, who would be entitled to receive a share of the sum distributed by the Queen – in practice, by the Keeper of the Privy Purse, Mr Peter Miles – among lesser members of the Royal Family as 'salary' for the share of public duties they undertake. In 1980, for instance, a total of £274,000 was divided between the late Princess Alice, the Duke of Kent, the Duke of Gloucester and Princess Alexandra.

The Civil List also specifically allots a pension to the Princess of Wales, at present fixed at £60,000 a year, should her husband die before he inherits the throne. But it is likely that Prince Charles will wish his wife to have no further involvement than that in the Royal Family's quota of public money. The revenues of the Duchy of Cornwall – in 1979, a net profit of £506,013 on an income of £2,658,726 – will be more than enough to maintain the expanded Wales household. At present, the Prince has adopted an arrangement instituted by the last Prince of Wales and Duke of Cornwall by which he returns half the Duchy's profits to the Treasury as a form of 'voluntary income tax'. He has always reserved the right to alter this arrangement upon his marriage, and may now see fit to keep a larger proportion to finance the extra staff, both private and professional, his marriage will entail. But he will certainly continue to surrender an annual percentage to the Treasury, as the present arrangement makes for extremely good public relations.

Diana, Duchess of Cornwall, will be the wife of one of Britain's leading landlords: the Duchy owns some 130,000 acres in nine counties, including such disparate tenancies as the oyster beds of the River Helford (leased to Mac Fisheries Ltd) and Dartmoor prison. The Prince has first claim on any porpoise or whale washed up on the Cornish beaches; he can, should he choose, extract a tithe of 300 puffins a year from the inhabitants of the Isles of Scilly; and may in any year exercise, as he did in 1973, his right to his seigneurial dues, to wit:

a load of firewood, a grey cloak, 100 old shillings, a pound of pepper, a hunting bow, a pair of gilt spurs, a pound of herbs, a salmon spear resembling Neptune's trident, a pair of falconer's gauntlets, and two greyhounds. (On enjoying this ancient ritual beside Launceston Castle eight years ago, the Prince promptly and graciously returned the greyhounds to their rightful owner, Lieutenant-Colonel John Molesworth-St Aubyn, and restored the rest of the booty to the Launceston Museum – 'ready', as he put it, 'for the next time'.)

The Duchy also owns forty-five acres in Kennington, London, always described in books and articles about Prince Charles as 'by far its most profitable asset'. The Kennington property has, if truth be told, shown substantial deficits in recent years, and has been described to the author by the secretary of the Duchy, Sir Anthony Gray, as 'a terrible drag on income'. The 850 London tenancies are held by, among others, the Prince's former nanny, Helen Lightbody, and the former Prime Minister, James Callaghan. The Duchy also owns Kennington Oval, the historic home of Surrey county cricket club and scene of an annual Test Match.

The Prince did not come into his Cornish inheritance until his twenty-first birthday, before which it was administered by the Queen on his behalf. Though much of its income was used to offset the Civil List, and a proportion spent on his education, the surplus was set aside to accumulate a nest-egg estimated at some £300,000 when Charles reached twenty-one. In subsequent years the Prince's expenditure – primarily on his staff and travelling expenses, but also on his sporting, motoring and other off-duty activities – has tended to be about twenty per cent less than his annual income from the Duchy, which has averaged between £200,000 and £250,000, rising to £306,382 in 1980. The surplus is invested on his behalf in a portfolio managed by a consortium of three City stockbroking firms. He himself is never aware of the scale or identity of the investments made in his name in this 'blind trust' – though he *does* pay normal income tax on its annual returns.

So the new Princess of Wales will hardly be kept in the poverty to which some of her predecessors became accustomed. Diana, indeed, has been bred to a gracious style of living; she may not bring with her the dowry which was once so vital a component of such princely marriages, but the Earl Spencer would always be able to help out his son-in-law in a crisis. Few British girls these days have fathers who can buy them £100,000 London flats in their 'teens. Althorp, the Spencer country seat where Prince Charles will be spending country weekends with his new in-laws, is in fact bigger than any of the Royal Family's country residences. Life at Highgrove may at first seem a little cramped to Lady Diana.

It certainly will when that first baby arrives. On the birth of the future heir to the throne in 1948, twelve extra typists had to be installed in the Palace to send out the cables bearing the news around the world – they had been pre-prepared, with a space left blank for the word 'Prince' or 'Princess' – and to answer the deluge of congratulatory mail. After announcing their engagement in February 1981, Prince Charles and Lady Diana had to enlist the help of twelve Wrens to handle the tidal waves of mail arriving at Buckingham Palace.

The Princess of Wales will already have at least one secretary to help with her appointments and her correspondence, and a team of four ladies-in-waiting (possibly including one or two of her former Chelsea flatmates) taking it in turns to help her out – unpaid – with various royal chores, and to escort her on her official public outings. She and her husband will already have a fairly large staff at Highgrove, given his need for two valets, several secretaries, security men, equerries and clutch of stable lads, on top of the 'downstairs' domestics. The baby's arrival will add a fleet of nursery staff, led by another in the distinguished tradition of formidable royal nannies. There will be a parade of eminences dropping by to pay their respects to the royal infant.

Prince Charles will no doubt hand on to his first son the christening present he himself received from his great-grandmother in 1948. 'I gave the baby', wrote Queen Mary in her diary, 'a silver gilt cup & cover which George III had given to a godson in 1780, so that I gave a present from my gt. grandfather to my great grandson 180 years later.' The christening will be a magnificent affair, probably in St George's Chapel at Windsor (though Charles was christened in Buckingham Palace, in the white and gold Music Room, because the Palace chapel had been destroyed in the Blitz – it is now the Queen's Gallery – and the King was too ill to travel to Windsor). At least eight royal godparents, or sponsors, will be chosen, and the child will be known by one of his father's subsidiary titles, of which there are plenty to choose from.

The happiest and most private period of the young couple's life together seems likely to be these first few years of their marriage, when they will be given the option of spending a period abroad. It is certainly true of Prince Charles's parents that they have never known such tranquil and joyous 'normality' as they did in the first two years after his birth, when they were able to spend some time together in the Mediterranean. Philip was second-in-command of HMS *Chequers*, serving under his uncle 'Dickie' Mountbatten, then flag officer commanding the first cruiser squadron in the Mediterranean. Mountbatten had a lush house on Malta, the Villa Guardamangia, overlooking the harbour, where Elizabeth flew to spend Christmas 1949 with her husband (leaving

Charles at home in the care of his grandparents and Aunt 'Margot' at San-dringham). It was here that Princess Anne was conceived.

After Anne's birth back in London, the following summer, there was another happy sojourn in the Med. On the very day of Anne's birth, 15 August 1950, her father had been gazetted Lieutenant-Commander and assigned, at last, his own command, the frigate *Magpie*. When his wife was able to join him, she was granted the privilege of living aboard the commander-in-chief's despatch vessel, HMS *Surprise*. It is a time they often recall with great nostalgia, as some of the Royal Family's most enjoyed private jokes date from the days when the two ships flashed each other cryptic messages:

Surprise to *Magpie*: 'Princess full of beans.'
Magpie to *Surprise*: 'Is that the best you can give her for breakfast?'

Their private code was to use Biblical texts; for instance:

Surprise to *Magpie*: Isaiah 33:23 ('Thy tacklings are loose.')
Magpie to *Surprise*: 1 Samuel 15:14 ('What meaneth this bleating of sheep?')

The fun and games ended all too suddenly in July 1951, when King George VI again fell ill, and the Duke of Edinburgh had to quit the Navy on indefinite leave. So fondly do the royal couple recall those halcyon days, however, that they will warmly urge Charles and Diana to spend some time abroad while they have the chance. There is one obvious option, about which the Prince himself has expressed great enthusiasm. Within a year or two of their marriage, Diana is likely to find herself the mistress of yet another splendid mansion: Government House, Canberra, Australia.

Despite recent denials from Buckingham Palace, we may feel confident that the Prince of Wales will succeed the present Governor-General of Australia, Sir Zelman Cowen, when he retires in the near future. Sir Zelman, an Australian lawyer and academic, has done much to calm ruffled feathers at both ends of the Anglo-Australian alliance since the dismissal of Gough Whitlam's Labour Government in 1975 by the then Governor-General, Sir John Kerr. The notion of Prince Charles assuming this role in the country of which he has proved himself so fond, and where he was in part educated, has been under discussion in royal circles since the early 1970s. But it was thought then that the Prince was still too young, and that further discussions would anyway have to await his marriage, the addition of a wife-cum-hostess being regarded in Buckingham Palace as indispensable in what is primarily a social and ceremonial job. The Whitlam–Kerr confrontation, and the major constitutional row which followed it, then brought the whole business too close to politics for princely comfort, and the idea was shelved *sine die*.

Since then, and since the likelihood late in 1980 that the Prince had at last found himself a bride, the matter has again been under active discussion, and has been raised by the Queen with her current Prime Minister, Margaret Thatcher, at their weekly Tuesday evening audiences. The Australian Prime Minister, Mr Malcolm Fraser, who has also discussed the matter with the British Foreign Secretary, Lord Carrington, has done nothing of late to quash the speculation. He was indeed specifically questioned on the possibility in the Australian Parliament in March 1981, after the author had revealed in an article in the *Observer* that the Royal Family had renewed its interest. Far from knocking any such idea on the head, Mr Fraser said that Australians would look forward to Prince Charles's appointment with 'very, very real enthusiasm'.

A public opinion poll taken at the time did not entirely bear out Mr Fraser's confidence. Published in the Sydney *Sun Herald*, it showed that twenty-eight per cent of those polled were in favour of Prince Charles becoming Governor-General and fifty-one per cent against, with twenty expressing no view. Those Australians with strong feelings on the subject are opposed in principle to anyone other than an Australian becoming Governor-General; as one government official put it in an unguarded moment: 'We don't want a bloody Pom foisted on us.' Mr Whitlam himself, though scarcely an impartial witness – and also the Prime Minister who abolished the British national anthem in Australia – expressed his opposition in a recent article in a leading Australian magazine, headlined 'Let Bonnie Prince Charlie Stay Over The Water'. Declared Mr Whitlam: 'If the Queen's heir were to become Governor-General, this would be taken as a sign that Australia is still subject to Britain. The appointment would bring no international benefits to Australia, but rather the contrary.'

It is nevertheless believed in London that the vast majority of Australians do not look on Prince Charles as 'a bloody Pom' – a Pom, perhaps, but an extremely popular and respected one – and that his appointment would, on the contrary to Mr Whitlam's argument, be taken at face value: as a reaffirmation of the especial regard in which Australia is held by the British Royal Family, and by Prince Charles in particular, as one of the major powers within the Commonwealth. The issue was very much to the fore during Prince Charles's most recent visit to Australia in April 1981, when Prince and Prime Minister again discussed the matter at some length, amid heightened public speculation. Mr Fraser's scenario has him winning an election in early 1983, and the Prince taking over as Governor-General almost immediately, with a maximum term of three years. Thus Mr Fraser hopes to guarantee the Prince a politically trouble-free period in Government House. Both were encouraged when the Leader of the Opposition, Mr Bill Hayden, publicly told the author that his opposition to the plan was purely personal, rather than official Labour Party policy. The constitutional dangers are very real, and Mr Fraser's scenario perhaps the only practical one. But it appears, at the time of writing, to have every chance of success.

Once the wrinkles are ironed out, therefore, the Royal Family feels confident that the appointment would be a popular one, that it would give the Prince of Wales invaluable experience in the role of a constitutional quasi-monarch, and that he and Diana would anyway relish – and deserve – a break from the ardours of their British routine. As fortune would have it, Sir Zelman's term in office is due to expire at the end of 1982, but could be extended a few months to suit the Prime Minister's electoral timing. It is highly likely that the Prince and Princess will have had their first child, and that Britons will not – after all the celebrations which will have attended that event – begrudge the absence of their young Royals for a while. The appointment is traditionally a five-year one, but it would be thought to be stretching the royal luck for the heir apparent to be absent from these shores for so long, quite apart from the political risks; they would return after a stint of some two or three years, perhaps bringing with them the first direct descendant of a British monarch – perhaps even the first future King – to have been born 'down under'.

So optimistic is the Royal Family about this plan that the years ahead, it seems possible, could also see Prince Andrew and possibly Prince Edward undertake a similar role in Australia or another Commonwealth country. Canada would be ideal for Prince Andrew, who went to school there for a while, assuming the constitutional difficulties of 1980–81 are resolved within the not too distant future. There has even been talk of Princess Anne and her husband undertaking a sojourn in one of the smaller Commonwealth countries, perhaps one of the Caribbean member-states, sometime in the next decade or two. The royal siblings have for some years now enjoyed a private joke amongst themselves that, as one of them somewhat overstated it: 'One day we'll carve up the world between us!'

CHAPTER SIX

Nine Princesses of Wales

BERTIE, Prince of Wales, was just sixteen years old when his parents, Queen Victoria and Prince Albert, began a Europe-wide search to find him a suitable bride. Everybody, according to Albert, was telling them: 'You must marry the Prince of Wales. Unless you do, he is lost.' They enlisted the aid of their daughter Vicky, the Princess Royal, herself already happily married to the future heir to the throne of Prussia.

'We must look out for princesses for Bertie,' the Queen wrote to Vicky. 'Oh! If you would find us one!' Victoria spelt out the royal requirements: 'Good looks, health, education, character, intellect and a good disposition, we want; great rank and riches, we do not.' That she must be a Protestant went without saying; that she must be good-looking was evident to Bertie's parents from his already roving eye. That was why they were marrying him off.

The Times helpfully printed a list of suggestions, while Vicky settled down beneath a chestnut tree with the *Almanach de Gotha*. But the list of suitable candidates was rather thin. 'Princesses', complained Vicky, 'do not spring up like mushrooms or grow upon trees.' Nevertheless, she set off to check those available, and was soon reporting back.

Princess Anna of Hesse had perhaps 'the fewest disadvantages', but she had 'an incipient twitching in her eyes ... a flat, narrow and upright forehead ... and a rather gruff, abrupt way of speaking'; her teeth were 'nearly all spoilt', she dressed 'terribly' and was prone to frowning. Not a very promising start.

There was Marie of Altenburg, but she too dressed badly and had 'a most disagreeable mother'. Marie of Hohenzollern-Sigmaringen would have done fine – 'quite lovely,' said Vicky – but she was Roman Catholic. The Princess of Sweden was too young, the Princess of Desau too old (with a family of 'bad reputation'). The Weimar girls were 'very nice, but delicate and not pretty', Marie of the Netherlands was 'clever and lady-like, but too plain and not strong'. Poor Princess Alexandrine of Prussia was '*not* clever or pretty'. Augusta of Meiningen was 'a very nice, clever, good girl' but still 'quite a child'.

Joint top of the initial shortlist was Princess Elizabeth of Weid. Victoria's chief adviser, Baron Stockmar, thought her 'dowdy', but Vicky was more encouraging. She was neither '*distinguée*' nor 'graceful', but she was blessed with 'a very fresh complexion and nice white teeth, a great many freckles and a mark of a leaf on one cheek but which does not show very much'. On the debit side, she had 'not a pretty nose and rather a long chin. . . . She is what you would call a strong, healthy-looking girl – nothing more – she does not look very lady-like and head not well dressed – whether she is clever or not I cannot say.' Elizabeth, who also was possessed of rather 'forward' manners, was finally pronounced 'odd'. And she was prone to coarse language: 'She says such things sometimes', reported Vicky, 'that I do not know which way to look.'

So all attention turned upon the other joint favourite, Princess Alexandra Caroline Marie Charlotte Louise Julie of Schleswig-Holstein-Sonderburg-Glucksburg, daughter of Prince Christian IX, the heir to the throne of Denmark. In December 1860, Vicky wrote to her mother: 'I have seen several people who have seen her of late – and who give such accounts of her beauty, her charms, her amiability, her frank natural manner and many excellent qualities. I thought it right to tell you all this in Bertie's interest, though I as a Prussian cannot wish Bertie should ever marry her.' It was unduly kind of Vicky to sing Alexandra's praises like this, as Denmark and Prussia were then locked in a bitter and long-standing territorial dispute over Schleswig-Holstein.

The Queen at first responded in kind. 'The beauty of Denmark is much against our wishes,' she wrote. 'What a pity she is who she is.' Alexandra, in Victoria's eyes, was the daughter of her mother, Princess Christian, a member of the House of Hesse-Cassel (of which Prince Albert took a dim view) and a sister of the Queen's marital aunt, the Duchess of Cambridge, a notorious social climber who had once tried to marry her own son to Victoria herself. There were other drawbacks: Victoria really wanted her son to marry a German; she did not wish to alienate the Prussian court, where lay her daughter's security and future prospects; and she disapproved strongly of the Danish court, where King Frederick VII openly lived 'in sin' and spent most of his time drunk.

Two months later, however, Victoria had received more glowing reports of Alexandra, along with the intelligence that the Tsar had his eye on her. 'It would be too dreadful', wrote Vicky, 'if this pearl were to go to the Russians.' Victoria rather agreed. There was, moreover, nobody else in Europe remotely suitable for Bertie. The Queen despatched her daughter to look over the Danish Princess, and by the summer Vicky was able to report:

> I never set eyes on a sweeter creature! She is lovely! Her voice, her walk, carriage and manner are perfect, she is one of the most lady-like and aristo-cratic looking people I ever saw! She is as simple and natural and unaffected as possible – and seems exceedingly well brought up. . . . She does not seem the least aware of her beauty and is very unassuming. . . . You may go far before you find another princess like Princess Alix – I know you and Papa would be charmed with her. . . . Oh, if only she was not a Dane and not related to the Hesses, I should say yes – she is the one a thousand times over. . . . The more I see of her, the more charming and attractive I think her.

On 24 September 1861, an ill-disguised sizing-up session took place in the cathedral at Speyer, where Bertie pretended to be visiting the Prussian army while the Princess and her family 'visited relations' at nearby Rumpenheim. Bertie and Alix were discreetly allowed to detach themselves from the rest of the group of royal sightseers, as the Bishop showed off his frescoes. Next day, the Prince of Wales wrote home about 'the young lady of whom I had heard so much; and I can now candidly say that I thought her charming and very pretty.' Back at Balmoral, however, he could only declare himself 'much pleased'. 'But as for being in love,' wrote his mother, much vexed, 'I don't think he can be.' Vicky too was outraged that Bertie had not succumbed to love at first sight. 'When I think of that sweet lovely flower – young and beautiful,' she wrote back, 'that even makes my heart beat when I look at her – which would make most men fire and flames – not even producing an impression enough to last from Baden to England. . . . If she fails to kindle a flame, none will ever succeed in doing so.'

Bertie was in a dither. He was riding out his parents' rage at his much-gossiped-about loss of innocence, when his fellow officers at the Curragh Camp had introduced a young actress of their acquaintance into his presence. Also, he had been so dragooned by his parents throughout his young life, that he was reluctant to be dragooned into marriage. He suddenly developed a 'fear of marrying and above all of having children'. Albert, characteristically, sat down at his memo pad and issued an ultimatum. The girl must be invited to stay at Windsor, and Bertie must immediately make up his mind. He would either fall in love with her at once, or he would bid her farewell forever. Any other behaviour 'would be most ungentlemanlike and insulting to the lady and her parents, and would bring disgrace upon you and us.'

It was a stark choice: marry her now, or never see her again. But Bertie was spared having to make it by his father's sudden death, supposedly of influenza contracted while rebuking Bertie over the episode at the Curragh. Victoria, mortified, blamed her son for her beloved husband's demise: 'Oh, that boy,' she wrote to Vicky, 'much as I pity, I never can or shall look at him without a shudder.' She also became more determined than ever that Bertie should marry Alix without delay. She decided 'to see the girl' for herself – to decide not if she was right for Bertie, but if 'she will suit me'. At the beginning of a pilgrimage to the late Albert's family in Coburg she dropped in on the Danish Royal Family, who were instructed to speak in hushed tones and on no account to laugh in her presence. Alexandra had the good sense to appear before Victoria in a plain black dress, wearing no jewellery, with her hair demurely in curls. 'Oh!' wrote Victoria in her diary, 'how he would have doted on her and loved her' – the highest praise the distraught widow of Windsor could bestow. Five days later, much to Prince Christian's surprise after the long and tortuous negotiations, Bertie fetched up in Brussels to ask for his daughter's hand in marriage.

Thus did Prince Charles's great-great-grandfather, the last but one Prince of Wales, find his bride. As his travelling companion, Sir Charles Phipps, wrote rather bluntly to the Queen in the same mailbag carrying her son's professions of undying love: 'It would be absurd to suppose that a real feeling of *love* could as yet exist for a person whom His Royal Highness has only seen in all for four hours.' But Bertie and Alix then spent four days together, and it seems that the seeds of genuine affection were quickly sown. 'You perhaps think', Alix later told one of her future sisters-in-law, 'that I am marrying your brother for his position. But if he was a cowboy I should love him just the same and marry no one else.' Baron Stockmar complained that it was 'an arranged marriage', by which he meant really to protest that he had not arranged it himself.

Charles and Diana may have enjoyed a more thoroughly modern courtship, but their snatched hours together – the press, rather than their parents, baying at their heels – contain some unhappy echoes of Bertie's whirlwind romance with Alix. One couple plighted their troth while strolling across the battlefield of Waterloo, the other while standing in the Parker-Bowleses' vegetable patch in the Cotswolds. But at least Charles had enjoyed the freedom to make his own choice, at almost twice the age at which Bertie had marriage thrust upon him. It is in their future, much more than in their brief life together so far, that Charles and Diana have much to learn from the example of his great-great-grandparents. Bertie and Alexandra were married nearly forty years before they became King and Queen. It seems entirely likely that Charles could reach at least the same age as Bertie, fifty-nine, before he inherits the throne.

Edward VII, against all the odds, turned out to be a wise, popular and respected King during his nine brief years on the throne. As a Prince of Wales for nearly sixty, he had dragged the monarchy into gambling and divorce scandals, taken a string of married women as his mistresses, drunk and played hard – supported, all the while, by a remarkable wife as loyal as she was long-suffering. 'I often think her lot is not an easy one,' Victoria wrote of Alexandra, 'but she is very fond of Bertie, though not blind.' The Princess of Wales was compelled to receive many of her husband's lovers – the wives of titled and fashionable men – among their guests at court, and over nearly five decades managed to do so without batting an eyelid. She would escort him to the pre-mières of plays starring his best-remembered passion, Lily Langtry, and would even sympathize with his tear-stained discards. After becoming King, Bertie still felt free to dally with society ladies; Alexandra, at the last, had the greatness of heart to invite her husband's final love, Mrs Alice Keppel, to join her beside his deathbed.

The prime cause of Bertie's irresponsibility was his mother's refusal to allow him any constitutional role while she remained alive. He had had a miserable childhood, force-fed an educational programme so rigorous that by the age of ten he was on the edge of a nervous breakdown. Prince Albert's instructions to Bertie's first tutor, an Eton master aptly named Henry Birch, had been quite simply to fashion 'an executive Governor of the State ... the repository of all the moral and intellectual qualities by which it is held together, and under the guidance of which it advances in the great path of civilization.' Even his other tutors had seen how disastrous the programme was proving. 'You will wear him out too early,' counselled his French master, Dr Voisin. 'Make him climb trees! Run! Leap! Row! In many things, savages are better educated than we are.' Albert would hear none of it.

The result was that Bertie reached maturity late, a backward and unworldly boy, still something of a nervous wreck. Victoria could not understand it. She decided her son was unfit to play any role in affairs of state, which, of course, only made matters worse. It was, interestingly enough, Lady Diana's great-great-grandfather, the fifth Earl Spencer, who again and again proposed to Victoria the one solution that Bertie craved, and that might have altered his demeanour as Prince of Wales. Lord-Lieutenant of Ireland in 1868–74, and again in 1882–85, Spencer tried to persuade the Queen that her son should replace him as a non-political Viceroy of Ireland, emphasizing the monarchy's commitment to the country by taking up residence there. It would do more good, he told her, 'than any political measure'. After ten years of vain pleading, despite the whole-hearted support of the Prime Minister, Gladstone, Spencer wrote to the Queen's secretary: 'I feel inclined to throw in the sponge, and retire to my plough in Northamptonshire.'

Elizabeth II has already proved herself, in all these respects, a shrewder and more kindly monarch – and mother – than Victoria. She and the Duke of Edinburgh had the good sense, early in Charles's life, to realize that there can be no specific 'training' for monarchy. Their son would have as 'normal' an education as possible, attending public schools with other children, and would otherwise simply observe them at work. As Charles himself has put it: 'I've learnt the way a monkey learns – by watching its parents.'

Even more important, the Queen has since involved the future King as broadly as possible in the functions of the constitutional monarchy. Where Victoria forbade Bertie ever to meet politicians, let alone talk shop with them, Elizabeth made Charles a Privy Councillor before his thirtieth birthday, enabling him to talk freely and on an entirely confidential basis with senior politicians of all parties. Even before that, she had ensured that Charles had access to Cabinet and other state papers, to keep abreast of political and diplomatic developments in Britain and around the world. Even her consort, Prince Philip, is not allowed that privilege.

In time, as Elizabeth II advances towards Victorian venerability, she will permit her son to take over many of the constitutional roles not reserved exclusively for the sovereign. He will become, in effect, a vice-monarch. And where Bertie was not even allowed to voice his opinion on the plan for him to reside in Dublin, it seems highly likely that Charles will spend a time as Governor-General of a major Commonwealth country, probably Australia.

For Lady Diana, therefore, the 'job' of Princess of Wales is likely to be rather more specific than it was for the hapless Alexandra. Bertie's Princess was excluded from many public and private occasions. She would accompany her husband on some of his public appearances; but was often left to her own devices, while the menfolk got up to manly things, in the royal residences or at their friends' country homes. Bertie was never the most attentive of husbands:

his wife bore him six children in five years, all of them with some complications because of her rheumatic condition, and he rarely danced attendance. Charles not merely lives in a more enlightened age, but is a more enlightened man. Diana may expect every fond attention. She will not, furthermore, have to look the other way during any sustained bouts of princely dalliance; Charles's views on the sanctity of marriage are as devoutly held as is his fundamentally religious attitude to the monarchy, which he regards as nothing less than a sacred duty.

He is the twenty-first Prince of Wales, Diana only the ninth Princess. Her predecessors have been a pretty star-cross'd crew suffering the vicissitudes of history and the whims of some none too worthy husbands. The only woman ever to attempt to claim the title of Princess of Wales in her own right was Mary Tudor, Henry VIII's only child after eighteen years of marriage to Catherine of Aragon. Her claim was always in legal doubt, but it was well and truly forfeit when her father divorced Catherine and declared Mary illegitimate.

The first Princess of Wales was Joan of Kent, the 'Fair Maid' of Kent, wife of Edward 'the Black Prince'. Thought to have been born in 1328 she was herself of royal blood, the daughter of Edmund, Earl of Kent, son of Edward I. Her mother was Margaret Wake, daughter of Lord Wake of Liddell. Joan was the first of two Princesses of Wales destined not to become Queen, as her husband, grandson of the first Prince of Wales (the future Edward II) was to die before his father, Edward III.

Joan was Edward's first cousin, and had grown up with him as the troubled court moved from Westminster to Windsor, from manor to manor. An independent-minded girl, she had at the age of twelve fallen in love with and secretly married one Thomas Holland, steward to the Earl of Salisbury. They told no one, and her husband was soon despatched to the war in France. Joan was thus in no position to demur when, a year later, she was married off to the Earl's heir, William Montagu. Described by Froissart as 'the most beautiful and loveable woman in the kingdom of England in her time', Joan, Countess of Salisbury, dominated court life and was rumoured to have many lovers. Her chief 'admirer', under the ambiguous rules of 'courtly love', was the King himself; it was in the midst of a court ball that Edward picked up Joan's garter, exclaiming to shocked courtiers, '*Honi soit qui mal y pense*' ('Evil to him who evil thinks'), thus providing the origin and the motto of Europe's most ancient order of chivalry, the Order of the Garter.

In 1347 Holland returned from the war and, not unreasonably, demanded his wife back. There ensued a mighty row, during which an enraged Salisbury imprisoned his wife in one of his castles while awaiting the verdict of the Pope, who ruled in Holland's favour. The Countess of Salisbury became Lady Holland (later inheriting, in her own right, the title of Duchess of Kent); she bore her husband five children, and accompanied him to France, where he negotiated the 1360 peace treaty at Bretigny and promptly died. In her early thirties, after an already action-packed life, Joan was again an eligible and desirable lady-in-waiting. Within nine months, fending off other suitors on all sides, she had married the Prince of Wales.

The hero of Crecy and Poitiers, Edward married Joan against his father's wishes. The King had hoped for a more useful political alliance, and may privately have resented his son's wedding with his former mistress (whom, according to some historical accounts, he had also once raped). But another dispensation from Rome overruled his objections, and Joan went off to hold luxurious and wanton court in Bordeaux with her new husband, whom she bore two sons. The first, Edward, died; the second, at the age of ten, became King Richard II.

Joan's beauty seems to have survived well into her fifties, when there are several accounts of her having been molested by her son's subjects during the Peasants' Revolt. In her later years she maintained courteous relations with her second husband, the Earl of Salisbury, and became a grandmother through her first marriage to Holland. Despite the unhappy fortunes of her son, the King, Joan's place in British history is doubly assured by her descendants on the Holland side, who seven generations later included King Edward IV of the House of York. She died on 7 August 1385, while hurrying to intercede with one son, the King, on behalf of another, John Holland.

It was 100 years before the embattled Royal Family of England created another Princess of Wales - Anne Neville, daughter of Warwick 'the King-maker', who at the age of fourteen was betrothed to Edward, Prince of Wales, in Angers Cathedral. Anne - of whom there are few contemporary accounts beyond the unreliable John Rous's 'seemly, able, beauteous ... full commendable, right virtuous, full gracious' - was a mere pawn in the long-drawn-out struggles between the Houses of Lancaster and York. Her brief and wretched lifespan, of less than thirty years, coincided almost exactly with that of the Wars of the Roses. She was Princess of Wales barely a year. Her husband Edward died in 1471 at the Battle of Tewkesbury, the end of the House of Lancaster's attempts to depose Edward IV in favour of Henry VI, and within the year she was remarried to Richard, Duke of Gloucester. Twelve years and sundry nefarious deeds later Anne was Richard III's Queen, as which she survived just two more years - dying, according to some accounts, at the hands of her husband, who was anxious to marry and have sons by Edward IV's heiress,

Elizabeth of York. Within five months Richard too lay dead, on Bosworth Field, and that same Elizabeth became Henry VII's Queen.

That eventful year, 1485, saw the birth in Spain of the Infanta Catalina, youngest daughter of King Ferdinand and Queen Isabella. The child was just two years old when Henry Tudor, keen to cement his friendship with Ferdinand, suggested an alliance with his own one-year-old son, Arthur, Prince of Wales. The two were married in 1501, when Arthur reached his fifteenth birthday. Great celebrations followed the wedding in St Paul's, but Henry was eager to appease the Welsh, and the young couple were quickly despatched to their bleak new residence at Ludlow Castle. Catherine of Aragon, Princess of Wales, watched as her Spanish retinue one by one fell prey to disease in a climate quite unlike that of Granada. As the March winds swept the Welsh landscape, bringing with them the dreaded 'sweating-sickness', Catherine too succumbed. She was too ill to nurse her husband when he also fell victim to the plague. On 4 April 1502, he died. The marriage, according to Catherine, had never been consummated.

On the death of the Queen the following year, the King himself briefly contemplated marrying his daughter-in-law, anxious to make a strategic match and breed more sons to ensure the succession. Arthur's younger brother Henry was not yet fifteen, so there was time to consider how best to exploit the young widow's presence at the British court. Ferdinand was horrified, hoping that a betrothal to the younger Henry would have sealed a long alliance between the two countries, and threatened to despatch an armada to bear Catherine home. So Henry VII abandoned his own claim, but still failed formally to confirm that she would one day marry his son. For seven years, until the King's death, Catherine remained a mere chattel in the diplomatic game – living at court as Princess of Wales, the first lady of the land, in abject poverty. On his accession in 1509, the young and glamorous King Henry VIII, one of the most erudite and eligible men in Europe, quickly made amends. Within two months of the old King's death, Catherine was Queen of England, a country seemingly launched on a golden age. The next few years, after those of uncertainty, brought her uncomplicated happiness. It was not, as history knows, to last.

It took almost two centuries, and the establishment of the House of Hanover on the British throne, for another Princess of Wales to inherit the title. (The Electress Sophia, impatient to succeed Queen Anne, occasionally called herself Princess of Wales, which, of course, she had no right to do.) Caroline of Ansbach, one of the most beautiful and cultured princesses in Europe, had married Prince George Augustus of Hanover in 1705. Her father, the Margrave of Ansbach, had thought it a second-best match, having wished her to marry the Archduke

Charles of Austria, second son of the Holy Roman Emperor; Caroline had, however, boldly rejected his proposal when the Habsburg family insisted she convert to Catholicism. George Augustus, like all the Hanoverians, proved a wayward husband, but Caroline sensibly tolerated his affairs and became the dominant partner in the marriage. Nine years after the wedding Queen Anne was dead, her father-in-law was King George I and her husband was Prince of Wales.

Life at the English court proved, to put it mildly, volatile. Father and son, King and Prince, were soon not speaking to each other, George I being furious with the Prince of Wales's support of the Whig cause against his own Tories. 'That she-devil,' he called the Princess of Wales, after she had openly criticized his political protégé, Robert Walpole. He refused to make his son Regent while he returned to Hanover, dubbing him instead 'Guardian of the Realm and Lieutenant', with none of the powers normally pertaining to a regency. In his absence, the Prince and Princess of Wales entertained in dazzling style at Hampton Court, surrounded by eager politicians looking to their future.

The King, on his return, was furious. After several more diplomatic incidents, he ordered the Prince of Wales arrested. His ministers refused to consign the heir apparent to the Tower, so he was placed instead under virtual house arrest at Leicester House in London. The Princess of Wales was offered the choice of remaining in the Palace with her children, or leaving them with the King. They were, she said, not 'a grain of sand' compared to her husband – but she was seen to weep copiously on leaving her daughters and baby son, who was mortally ill.

At Leicester House, the Waleses continued to maintain a 'junior court' of magnificent style and play host to leaders of the political opposition. Shrewdly, the Princess saw that the way to reconciliation with her father-in-law – and reunion with her children – was through Walpole, who had become the dominant figure of the day. Despite her initial mistrust of him, she began to develop an alliance between the future First Lord of the Treasury and the Prince of Wales, who as ever was too busy with his various affairs to notice his wife's manipulation of him. They did to some extent make up their differences, but Caroline was still allowed only limited access to her children, and again blamed Walpole. Her husband too became enraged with him, as he began to entice members of the 'Leicester House set' away to the greater power and respectability of the King's court.

At the last, it was Walpole's unparalleled political power which enforced another reconciliation. When George I died in 1727, and his long-suffering son became King George II, Walpole was the only man who could keep the Commons loyal. Caroline again cultivated him, and with her support – and the King's benign neglect – he accrued the unprecedented powers which led to his becoming known as Britain's first Prime Minister. It was an open secret, for all the King's efforts, who really ran the country; as a contemporary rhyme had it:

> You may strut, dapper George, but 'twill all be in vain;
> We know 'tis Queen Caroline, not you, that reign ...
> Then if you would have us fall down and adore you,
> Lock up your fat spouse as your dad did before you.

Caroline made life as difficult for the new Prince of Wales, her son Frederick Louis, as had George I for her husband. Frederick, then twenty-one, was peremptorily summoned over from Hanover, where several offers of marriage had already fallen through. Now he was besieged by English matrons wishing to make future Queens of their daughters – notably the old Duchess of Marlborough, who pushed forward her grand-daughter, one Lady Diana Spencer. Despite the additional offer of a dowry of £100,000, the match, as we have seen, was not to be.

George II, meanwhile, had spent one of his periodic visits to Hanover inspecting Princess Augusta of Saxe-Gotha; he recommended her, with no particular enthusiasm, to his son, who, with no particular enthusiasm, concurred. Their relationship had become a mirror-image of that of the King and his own father: Frederick's 'Leicester House set' was annoying his father, who was denying him any political role, least of all that of Regent during his trips home. Frederick, a shrewd and cultivated fellow with an eye to the main chance, sought to make amends by marrying whomever his parents wished. He had mistresses enough to compensate for whatever disappointment might result.

Augusta, then seventeen, arrived in London in April 1736. One of the first courtiers to see her, the Earl of Egmont, described her as 'about the Prince's height, much pitted from the smallpox, and had a great colour from the heat of day and the hurry and surprise.... But she has a peculiar affability of behaviour and a very great sweetness of countenance, mixed with innocence, cheerfulness and sense.'

Caroline, by contrast, described Augusta as 'far from beautiful' with 'a wretched figure' and hair 'of a sheep's colour', while conceding that she had 'pretty eyes and a good mouth' and was 'anxious as a good child to please'. But she still had no higher an opinion of her son; after the wedding, she wrote of Augusta: 'Poor creature, if she were to spit in my face, I should only pity her for being under such a fool's direction, and wipe it off.' Frederick further annoyed his parents by conspiring with the parliamentary opposition to increase his financial allowance. When Caroline lay dying, not long after, in 1737, she refused him permission to visit her.

The tiresome family feuds of the early Hanoverians soon brought England to fever pitch. George was an old King, Frederick and Augusta an immensely popular couple-in-waiting. Frederick became a potent political force, leading concerted opposition to Walpole, who eventually fell in 1742. It was the prelude, as Frederick and his supporters thought, to his imminent accession to the throne, with the friendly Pelham Government in office. For all his scheming, for all his happy marriage with Augusta, for all the birth of the future King George III and his siblings, it was not to be. In March 1751, at the age of forty-four, he died of a cold caught while gardening at Kew. Augusta refused to believe it, remaining beside his corpse for hours in expectation of his recovery, even delaying the funeral for three weeks just in case. His epitaph – now famous, but grossly unfair to so accomplished a man – summed up the British people's impatience with the uncivil wars between each successive Prince of Wales and his father:

> Here lies poor Fred,
> Who was alive and is dead;
> Had it been his father,
> I had much rather;
> Had it been his brother,
> Still better than another;
> Had it been his sister,
> No one would have missed her;
> Had it been the whole generation,
> Still better for the nation;
> But since 'tis only Fred,
> Who was alive and is dead,
> There's no more to be said.

Lord Hervey, an enemy of Frederick and in other ways an unreliable witness, wrote of the Prince an epitaph which was in its way quite generous, while at the same time speaking volumes of the Hanoverian Princes and Princesses of Wales: that Frederick 'always used to say a Prince should never talk to any woman of politics, or make use of any wife but to breed; and that he would never make the ridiculous figure his father had done in letting his wife govern him or meddle in his business.'

Augusta, ever the shrewd diplomat, wrote to her father-in-law, the King: 'I throw myself, together with my children, at your feet. We commend ourselves, Sire, to your paternal love and protection.' The King hurried round, to find

Bertie marries Alix in 1863: Victoria looks down in sorrow from the balcony in St George's Chapel, Windsor, and gazes at a bust of her dead husband as the newlyweds show their joy.

The Prince of Wales, the future King George v, marries his elder brother's sometime fiancée, Princess May of Teck; their son and heir, now the exiled Duke of Windsor, marries Mrs Wallis Simpson, 'the woman I love'.

Lady Elizabeth Bowes-Lyon leaves her London home to marry the Duke of York; they pose
for the formal wedding picture, little knowing they will soon be King and Queen.

Princess Elizabeth arrives at the Abbey for her wedding; the Princess and her husband, Lieutenant Philip Mountbatten RN, pose for posterity.

OPPOSITE: At a time of national austerity, Britain celebrates 'a flash of colour'. The Archbishop of Canterbury has issued a special royal wedding licence.

Geoffrey Francis

by Divine Providence Archbishop of Canterbury Primate of All England and Metropolitan by Authority of Parliament lawfully empowered for the purposes herein written TO Our well beloved in Christ Her Royal Highness The Princess Elizabeth Alexandra Mary, Daughter of His most Gracious Majesty The King and Lieutenant Philip Mountbatten R.N. Son of His late Royal Highness Prince Andrew of Greece G.C.V.O. and of Her Royal Highness Princess Andrew, R.R.C. Health in our Lord God Everlasting WHEREAS His Most Excellent Majesty George the Sixth by the Grace of God, of Great Britain, Ireland and the British Dominions beyond the Seas King, Defender of the Faith, was graciously pleased to signify His Royal Consent to your contracting the Holy Estate of Matrimony by His Letters Patent under the Great Seal of the Realm in the words following... to wit... "George the Sixth by the Grace of God of Great Britain Ireland and the British Dominions beyond the Seas King, Defender of the Faith to all to whom these Presents shall come sendeth Greeting. Whereas by an Act of Parliament intituled "An Act for the better regulating the future Marriages of the Royal Family" it is amongst other things enacted "that no descendant of the body of His late Majesty King George the Second Male or Female (other than the issue of Princesses who have married or may hereafter marry into foreign families) shall be capable of contracting Matrimony without the previous consent of His Majesty His Heirs or Successors, signified under the Great Seal and declared in Council" Now know Ye that we have consented and do by these Presents signify Our consent to the contracting of Matrimony between Our Most Dearly Beloved Daughter Her Royal Highness The Princess Elizabeth Alexandra Mary and Lieutenant Phillip Mountbatten, R.N. Son of His late Royal Highness Prince Andrew of Greece, G.C.V.O. and of Her Royal Highness Princess Andrew, R.R.C. In witness whereof We have caused Our Great Seal to be affixed to these Presents GIVEN at Our Court at Buckingham Palace the thirty first day of July One thousand nine hundred and forty seven in the eleventh year of Our Reign" And whereas at His Majesty's Court at Buckingham Palace on the thirty first day of July One thousand nine hundred and forty seven present The King's Most Excellent Majesty in Council His Majesty was pleased to declare His Consent to the said Contract of Matrimony and caused His said Consent to be signified under the Great Seal and to be entered in the Books of the Privy Council And whereas Our Sovereign Lord, the King hath been pleased to make issue and direct to Us His Royal Warrant in this behalf in the words following... to wit... "Our Will and Pleasure is that you grant your Licence for solemnizing a Marriage between Our Most Dearly Beloved Daughter Her Royal Highness The Princess Elizabeth Alexandra Mary and Lieutenant Phillip Mountbatten. R.N. Son of His late Royal Highness Prince Andrew of Greece, G.C.V.O. and of Her Royal Highness Princess Andrew, R.R.C. notwithstanding the usual Oaths be not taken previous to the granting of such Licence We being well assured there is not any Impediment of Pre-Contract consanguinity affinity or other lawful cause to hinder the said Marriage nor any suit depending in any Court touching any Contract or Marriage of either of the said Parties and you are further to taken care that the said Marriage be publicly solemnized And for so doing this shall be your Warrant Given at Our Court at Buckingham Palace the thirty first day of July One thousand nine hundred and forty seven in the eleventh year of Our Reign" We therefore in Obedience to the said Royal Warrant of Our Sovereign Lord the King to Us directed in this behalf as aforesaid DO so far as in Us lies and the Laws of this Realm allow by these Presents Graciously Give and Grant Our Licence and Faculty as well to you the Parties contracting as to all Christian People willing to be present at the solemnization of the said Marriage to celebrate and solemnize such Marriage at any time in any Church or Chapel or other meet and convenient place by any Bishop of this Realm or by the Rector Vicar Curate or Chaplain of such Church or Chapel or by any other Minister in Holy Orders of the Church of England Given under the Seal of Our Office of Faculties in the City of Westminster this twenty second day of September in the year of Our Lord One thousand nine hundred and forty seven and in the third year of Our Translation.

H. T. A. Dashwood
Registrar

Princess Margaret marries a 'commoner', Antony Armstrong-Jones; thirteen years later, Princess Anne marries another, Captain Mark Phillips. All and sundry sign Princess Anne's wedding certificate.

19 73	Marriage solemnized at	Westminster Abbey	in the	Close	of St Peter: Westminster	in the County of	London		
No.	When Married	Name and Surname	Age.	Condition.	Rank or Profession.	Residence at the time of Marriage.	Father's Name and Surname.	Rank or Profession of Father.	
320	14th. November 1973	Mark Anthony Peter Phillips	25	Bachelor	Captain: 1st The Queens Dragoon Guards	Mount House. Great Somerford Chippenham. Wiltshire.	Peter William Garside Phillips	Major: M.C. Company Director	
		Anne Elizabeth Alice Louise Mountbatten - Windsor	23	Spinster	Princess of the United Kingdom of Great Britain and Northern Ireland	Buckingham Palace	His Royal Highness The Prince Philip	Duke of Edinburgh K.G. O.M.	

Married in Westminster Abbey according to the Rites and Ceremonies of the Established Church by Special Licence by me.

This Marriage was solemnized between us, Mark Phillips / Anne

+ Michael Cantuar:

in the presence of us :—

Elizabeth R   Philip   Anne Phillips   Eric S. Abbott Dean.

Elizabeth R   Alice Page. Peter Phillips   Sarah Phillips   Edward   Katharine

Charles.   Andrew   Eric Crouch   Margaret   Alexandra Michael   Alice

Edward.   Sarah   Snowdon   Angus Ogilvy   Richard

Linley   Mountbatten of Burma   Birgitte

George St. Andrews.   Helen Windsor.

The wedding of Princess Anne and Mark Phillips at Westminster Abbey in 1973; and the altar of St Paul's, where the Prince of Wales will marry Lady Diana Spencer on 29 July, 1981.

All smiles after the Privy Council has approved the wedding . . . and kisses—from an admiring schoolboy, and from Prince Charles, before he leaves on a six-week round-the-world trip.

Augusta and her two sons, George and William, kneeling before him in a chamber draped with black curtains. The past was forgotten; the King wept with them, and the elder son, George, at the age of twelve, was created Prince of Wales.

Such was Augusta's political prowess that she connived with senior politicians to persuade the King to appoint her Regent, while awaiting her son's majority, rather than his favourite son, 'Butcher' Cumberland. 'Princess Prudence', as the gossip Horace Walpole dubbed her, meanwhile formed a lasting alliance with John Stuart, Earl of Bute. He may or may not have been Augusta's lover – the weight of contemporary evidence suggests that he was – but Bute certainly became a lasting force in the lives of the widowed Princess and her son, the future King George III.

In 1755, when the new Prince of Wales was seventeen years old, George II proposed that his grandson marry the Princess Sophia Caroline of Brunswick-Wolfenbuttel. The Princess of Wales, as Augusta was still known, had no desire for her son to marry as smart and dominating a young woman as the Princess of Brunswick was reputed to be. She proposed a match with her own niece, Frederica Louisa of Gotha, and declared the Princess Sophia Caroline 'deformed and ugly'. The King, in turn, declared himself 'bewolfenbuttled'. A compromise was eventually struck on George's behalf in the shape of Princess Charlotte Sophia of Mecklenburg-Strelitz, young, ugly and appropriately dim, who married Augusta's son when he had already become King George III.

Augusta died in 1772, in misery, having seen her younger children fall into chaos and disarray. The judgment of her old friend and rival, Walpole, was that she had neglected them for the sake of the future King. But George's relationship with Bute was the true measure of his relations with his mother. He saw the now discredited politician when it suited him, and turned a blind eye to Augusta's continued association with Bute. Once again, a Prince of Wales-become-King had proved even more mettlesome than his parent had expected of him.

It was Princess Caroline of Brunswick-Wolfenbuttel, the niece of George's sometime intended, who was to become the next Princess of Wales. George's heir, the future King George IV, lived up with a vengeance to his Hanoverian ancestry: he married, in secret, in 1785, a Mrs Maria Fitzherbert, who was not merely a commoner but also a Catholic. The 1701 Act of Settlement, by which the family's claim to the throne was legally established, had forbidden any Catholic marriages; and the Royal Marriages Act of 1772, instituted by his father, had legally invalidated any marriages, without the King's permission, by any member of his family under the age of twenty-five. (The Prince was twenty-three.) He already had many mistresses, and at least one child by Mrs Fitzherbert, by the time Princess Caroline was shipped over to be his bride. George's then favourite, Lady Jersey, took pains to meet the Princess and cover her in make-up to ensure she would not impress; the courtier sent to escort her, James Harris, Earl of Malmesbury, was already at the end of his tether. On the voyage over, he had attempted to improve the Princess's knowledge of hygiene, which was clearly not her strong point. She swore, was 'vulgar', 'noisy' and seemingly unwilling to better herself. Her own mother wrote of her:

> She has much vanity, and though not void of wit, she has but little principle. . . .
> It is quite essential that she should fear as that she should love him. It is of the
> utmost importance that he should keep her closely curbed; that he should
> compel her respect for him. Without this she will assuredly go astray.

On his first glimpse of Caroline, the Prince said to Malmesbury: 'Harris, I am not well, pray get me a glass of brandy.' The Princess, in turn, was not at her best; she spoke sneeringly of Lady Jersey, whose 'position' she had been quick to judge, and expressed open disappointment at the corpulence and florid complexion of her husband-to-be. They were married next day. 'Judge what it is', Caroline told a friend in later years, 'to have a drunken husband on one's wedding day, and one who spent the greater part of his bridal night under the grate, where he fell and I left him. . . . If anybody were to say to me at this moment, would you live your life over again or be killed, I would choose death.'

Not a very auspicious start. George remained in considerable debt, largely as a result of gambling and whoring, and Caroline did little to assuage his very public embarrassment. She bore him the statutory child, a daughter named Charlotte Augusta, but he promptly made a will in which he cut his wife off with the traditional shilling. George petitioned for a separation, to which Caroline readily acceded. There ensued the ultimate Hanoverian farce: the hounding of the Princess of Wales, her eventual flight from the country, her progress across Europe and what is now called the Middle East in the arms of many a paramour, the untimely death of her daughter – and the unlikely and unsought dénouement of her being declared Queen on the death of her husband's father. She returned to England, where a 'trial' in the House of Lords failed to accept her husband's case for a royal divorce. She was, nevertheless, allowed no part in his Coronation in 1821. It was the greatest relief to King George that his 'wife' had the good sense of timing to die three weeks later, after being taken ill at a Drury Lane first night. Neither emerges with much credit from the entire episode.

King George IV outlived Caroline by ten years, but bred no further (legitimate) heirs, and was succeeded on the throne by his brother William IV, who was in turn succeeded in 1837 by his niece Victoria. Thus did Britain bid a final and none too fond farewell to the Hanoverians.

The House of Saxe-Coburg-Gotha, renamed the House of Windsor in 1917, produced the last two Princesses of Wales before Lady Diana. They were also, along with the present Queen Mother, the two most substantial Queen Consorts of modern times. Alexandra, wife of King Edward VII, we have already met; her daughter-in-law, Princess May of Teck, was to prove no less formidable a figure.

Victoria Mary, daughter of a German Duke and a grand-daughter of King George III, was the first Princess of Wales in 450 years to have enjoyed a predominantly English upbringing. She was born in 1867 in Kensington Palace, where her parents had taken refuge from the wars in Europe. She grew up in White Lodge, Richmond, on the periphery of Queen Victoria's family circle, and 'came out' in London society in 1886. Victoria disapproved of Mary's 'fast' mother, but thoroughly warmed to the correct behaviour of her eldest daughter, whom she pronounced 'a very nice girl, *distinguée*-looking, with a pretty figure'. Although she was of the second rank of European royalty, entitled a 'Serene' rather than a 'Royal' Highness, the Queen approved of her enough to consider her a suitable match for her son's heir.

The Prince of Wales's elder son was Prince Albert Victor, known to his family as 'Eddy'. He was a slow and dissolute youth, a great disappointment to his parents, who much preferred his younger brother George. Eddy's father called him 'Collar and Cuffs': he was all neck and wrists. He was, moreover, not merely the libertine his father had been before him; he was unruly, a frequenter of brothels, a known homosexual, in the habit of disappearing to the seedier reaches of the East End after dark. (To this day, theories survive that Eddy was Jack the Ripper.) For once, Queen Victoria and her son were agreed: Eddy's only chance of salvation was 'a good sensible wife with some considerable character'. Princess May filled the bill. Eddy proposed to her in December 1891, was accepted – and a month later, at the age of twenty-seven, was dead of pneumonia.

George was distraught. He had never been particularly close to his brother, though in death he found him irreplaceable: 'No two brothers', he wrote to his mother, Alexandra, 'could have loved each other more than we did. It is only now that I have found out how deeply I loved him!' More to the point, George was in despair at the prospect of having to give up his naval career, now that he must take over his brother's duties as heir to the throne. By his own confession, he was entirely ill-equipped for the role, with an education 'below that of the average country gentleman educated at a public school', and a complete ignorance of domestic and foreign affairs. His main interests were yachting, shooting, stamp-collecting and the management of his father's Sandringham estates.

It is extraordinary how often, in the history of British Kings and Queens, it is the younger brother who has eventually succeeded to the throne. (Even in the last generation, the Duke of York had no expectation of becoming King when he married Lady Elizabeth Bowes-Lyon.) Among Princes of Wales, two of those younger brothers have also inherited the brides once intended for their prematurely deceased siblings. There was a certain inevitability about the fact that May's attachment to Prince Eddy should be transferred to his brother George, and that George should find in May all the comfort and reassurance he needed in this, his hour of greatest crisis. They were married the following year.

May was Princess of Wales for only nine years, during her father-in-law's brief reign as King Edward VII; but as Princess and later as George's Queen Mary she set a formidable example, within living memory, for Diana to follow. Prince Charles, as a child, played at Mary's footstool; she lived to see one son renounce the throne, and the next die a premature death after rallying the nation around the throne during another devastating war. The matriarch of the House of Windsor until her death shortly before Elizabeth II's Coronation, Queen Mary remains the model for the conduct of British royal ladies to this day. Several members of the present Royal Family, in moments of stress, have confessed to sensing her beady eye bearing down on them.

Diana, Princess of Wales, is thus the ninth in a line of royal Princesses whose fortunes have not always proved happy and glorious. She is likely to pass many more years as Princess than as Queen; her husband-to-be is well aware of this, and has already fashioned his own life to more constructive ends than many previous Princes of Wales. Lady Diana, who has already, during their engagement, displayed her own spirit of independence, will wish to be seen to be an active Princess of Wales, using her office for more than merely ceremonial purposes. It will take her a few years to 'learn the ropes', as her father-in-law puts it; she is likely to spend them as a mere adjunct to her husband, like so many Princesses before her. In time, however, Diana will wish to emulate the example of her greatest predecessor, Alexandra, who proved not merely the mainstay of her husband's stormy life, but an ever more popular – if eccentric – first lady of the realm.

CHAPTER SEVEN

Two Royal Weddings: 1947 and 1981

'I SUPPOSE one thing led to another,' recalls Prince Philip, Duke of Edinburgh. 'I suppose I began to think about it seriously, oh, let me see now, when I got back in 'forty-six and went to Balmoral. It was probably then that we, that it became, you know, that we began to think about it seriously, and even talk about it.'

The future Queen Elizabeth II fell in love with the first man she ever met. Princess Elizabeth was just thirteen when she accompanied her father, King George VI, on a visit to his alma mater, the Royal Naval College at Dartmouth, in July 1939. There was a double epidemic of mumps and chickenpox among the cadets, so she and her sister Margaret were confined to the house of the commanding officer, Admiral Sir Frederick Dalrymple-Hamilton, where the young rating assigned to entertain them was 'a fair-haired boy, rather like a Viking, with a sharp face and piercing blue eyes'. He was the eighteen-year-old Prince Philip of Greece, nephew of her father's great friend Dickie Mountbatten.

The description is that of the young Princesses' governess, Miss Marion

Crawford ('Crawfie'), who has recalled the day in more detail than anyone else present can muster:

> She never took her eyes off him the whole time. At the tennis courts I thought
> he showed off a good deal, but the little girls were much impressed. Lilibet
> said, 'How good he is, Crawfie! How high he can jump!' He was quite polite
> to her, but did not pay her any special attention. . . .'

Philip entertained them again all the next day, which climaxed in 'several platefuls of shrimp, and a banana split, among other trifles. . . . To the little girls, a boy of any kind was always a strange creature out of another world. Lilibet sat pink-faced, enjoying it all very much. . . .' At the end of the day, a huge flotilla of small boats surrounded the royal yacht, *Victoria and Albert*, and escorted her down the river and out to sea. The King began to fear for their safety, and ordered that they be signalled to turn back. One solitary rower, however, struggled manfully to keep up in the yacht's wake, exasperating the King ('The damned young fool,' he is supposed to have exclaimed), but delighting Princess Elizabeth, who 'watched him fondly through an enormous pair of binoculars'. Dickie Mountbatten at last bellowed to his gallant nephew to head back to shore.

Just two months later Britain and Germany were at war, and the young couple separated by Philip's active service. He maintained a 'cousinly correspondence' with Elizabeth, and seized any chance while on leave to visit her family at Windsor. The King, apparently unaware of the feelings of his young daughter, enjoyed hearing Philip's first-hand accounts of the war in the Mediterranean. It was the nearest he himself could get to active service in his beloved Navy.

Within two years of that first meeting at Dartmouth, when Elizabeth was still only fourteen and Philip nineteen, Henry ('Chips') Channon recorded in his diary: 21 January 1941: 'An enjoyable Greek cocktail party. Philip of Greece was there. He is extraordinarily handsome. . . . He is to be our Prince Consort, and that is why he is serving in our Navy.'

Channon was jumping the gun a bit, but his source was a good one: Princess Nicholas of Greece, the mother of Princess Marina, Duchess of Kent. If the matter was under discussion in royal circles, she of all people would be sure to know. In later years, Prince Philip looked back on the episode rather casually, in conversation with his biographer, Basil Boothroyd:

> It had been mentioned, presumably, that he is 'eligible, he's the sort of person
> she might marry'. I mean, after all, if you spent ten minutes thinking about
> it – and a lot of these people spent a great deal more time thinking about it
> – how many obviously eligible young men, other than people living in this

country, were available? Inevitably I must have been on the list, so to speak. But people only had to say that for somebody like Chips Channon to go one step further and say it's already decided, you see what I mean?

Whatever discussions there may have been, there was also an implicit recognition that nothing could be decided while the country was at war. Philip distinguished himself at the Battle of Matapan, and continued to pay polite visits to the Royal Family, a relative rather than a suitor, during his leaves. By Christmas 1943, however, Elizabeth's feelings for him had become totally undisguised. Philip sat in the front row as she and her sister tripped the light fantastic in the annual Windsor pantomime – that year, *Aladdin*. 'I have never known Lilibet more animated,' wrote Crawfie. 'There was a sparkle about her none of us had ever seen before. Many people remarked on it.' Whatever she and Philip said to each other in private, their correspondence grew more intense, and by March 1944 his older cousin, King George of Greece, had approached George VI on his behalf. The King dashed their hopes. 'We both think she is too young for that now,' he replied, 'as she has never met any young men her own age. . . . I like Philip. He is intelligent, has a good sense of humour & thinks about things in the right way.' But any such talk was, as yet, premature. 'P. had better not think about it any more for the present.'

Even when the war ended, the King would not permit his daughter to be confident about her feelings for Philip. He launched a series of Palace dances in her honour, inviting all the eligible young men of the kingdom, and the newspapers were soon full of rumours about her imminent engagement to Hugh Fitzroy, Earl of Euston, or Charles Manners, Duke of Rutland, both type-cast for the job: twenty-four years old, Eton, Cambridge, now officers in the Grenadier Guards. Queen Mary, who was aware of her grand-daughter's true feelings, watched the whole process with some amusement, referring to the parade of bachelors as 'the Body Guard'. She told her friend Lady Airlie that the King and Queen wanted their daughter 'to meet more men', and Lady Airlie herself speculated in her diary that the King 'was secretly dreading the prospect of an early engagement for her'. Queen Mary herself, her lady-in-waiting reminded her, had fallen in love at Elizabeth's age, and how that had lasted! Yes, said the old Queen, 'Elizabeth seems to me that kind of girl. She would always know her own mind. There's something very steadfast and determined in her.' When one member of the family made mock of Philip's education at Gordonstoun, calling it 'a crank school with theories of complete social equality where the boys were taught to mix with all and sundry', he was rewarded with one of Queen Mary's most devastating glares. That, she rebuked him, would prove 'useful'.

But there was another problem. British troops were actively engaged in the Greek civil war, which was delaying Philip's long-cherished ambition to become a naturalized British subject. For the British Royal Family to endorse that now would put them in the invidious position of appearing to abandon the Greek royalists' cause as hopeless. George VI would hear none of it. But his daughter was, as Queen Mary had said, both determined and independent-minded. When, during that Balmoral summer of 1946, Prince Philip of Greece proposed to her, she accepted him at once.

It was to be nearly a year before the King would allow them to make their engagement public. Total secrecy was, indeed, the only basis on which he was prepared to accept what had clearly become a *fait accompli*. It was not that the King in any way opposed Philip as his daughter's future consort; quite the reverse. But there were continuing political problems, with Britain in xenophobic mood; George was perhaps an ever-possessive father, not wishing to part with his daughter so soon; and he had already announced a major royal tour of South Africa, on which he was anxious for Elizabeth to accompany him. So there could be no announcements for a while; the couple were obliged to maintain a discreet silence while Buckingham Palace issued categorical denials that they had become engaged.

The Princess celebrated her twenty-first birthday in South Africa, which she marked by a radio address on the subject of 'duty'. On their return, it was the Home Secretary of the day, Chuter Ede, who suggested that Prince Philip might adopt the family name of Mountbatten, the anglicized version of his mother's family name, Battenberg. His uncle Dickie was delighted. Once Prince Philip of Greece and Denmark had shed both his name and all his titles, becoming plain Lieutenant Philip Mountbatten RN, it was finally agreed that the royal engagement could be announced.

When it was, on 10 July 1947, an opinion poll showed that the King's fears had been well-founded: forty per cent of those polled opposed the marriage on the grounds that Philip was a foreigner. Such opposition soon ebbed, however, when a bruised and battered post-war Britain geared up for a much-needed piece of royal pageantry. The news of the engagement, said Winston Churchill, was 'a flash of colour on the hard road we have to travel'.

In those days of bitter austerity, when a lavish royal event might have caused resentment, the Commons proved more generous than it occasionally does today. It voted the young couple £60,000 a year in allowances from the Civil List, and a further £50,000 for the renovation of Clarence House. Fifteen hundred gifts arrived from all over the world, including a silver ashtray from General and Mrs Eisenhower, and a personally spun piece of cloth – described with distaste by Queen Mary as 'a loin cloth' – from Mahatma Gandhi. The week before the wedding, set for 20 November, saw the biggest gathering of royalty, including many a dethroned exile, in a century. 'A week of gaiety such as the court had not seen for years,' wrote Lady Airlie. 'There were parties at St James's Palace to view the wedding presents, a royal dinner party for all the foreign royalties, and an evening party at Buckingham Palace which seemed after the years of austerity like a scene out of a fairy tale.' 'Saw many old friends,' Queen Mary recorded in her diary. 'I stood from 9.30 till 12.15 a.m.!!! Not bad for eighty.'

Even Lord Beaverbrook's *Daily Express*, which had traditionally been hostile to the Mountbatten family, wrote in a leading article that the engagement

> heightens the ordinary man's sense of history. It enables him to project the past into the future and to see the rich pattern of events.... This age into which Princess Elizabeth was born contains no dream of El Dorado such as inspired the Tudor sea-dogs and the Victorian pioneers. Instead, it has been filled with the nightmare of violent change and of misery in the world of a scale unimagined before.

The rest of the national press waxed lyrical.

The Princess, like any other post-war bride, had been saving her clothing coupons for her bridal gown, and received the statutory extra two hundred contributed by the Government to all bridal trousseaux. Many women around the country, however, sent her extra coupons out of their own allowance: the Princess was obliged to return them, as it was illegal to transfer clothing coupons, but she attached a personally written note of thanks with each.

Norman Hartnell, the royal dress designer, had sought inspiration in the National Gallery, where he dreamt up 'a Botticelli figure in clinging ivory silk, trailed with jasmine, similax, syringa and small white blossoms'. He white-washed the windows of his studio, and had his assistant sleep on a camp bed across the door, to prevent any sneak previews or commercial imitations. When the dress was finally unveiled, he was declared by one fashion writer to have

> shown himself no mean poet. In a design based on delicate Botticelli curves, he has scattered over the ivory satin garlands of white York roses carried out in raised pearls, entwined with ears of corn minutely embroidered in crystal. By the device of reversed embroidery he has alternated star flowers and orange blossom, now tulle on satin and now satin on tulle, the whole encrusted with pearls and crystals.

The day itself dawned a rainy one, but huge crowds lined the route from the Palace to Westminster Abbey, which had been decorated with flags, bunting and banners bearing the giant initials 'E' and 'P'. Inside the Palace, there were the usual last-minute flaps. The bride's tiara broke as it was being placed on her head, and a jeweller had to rush it off for repairs. The pearls due to adorn the Princess's neck (a present from her parents) were late arriving from St James's Palace, where they had been on display among the wedding gifts; the hapless footman despatched to collect them had underestimated the scale of the crowds blocking his progress. The bride's bouquet was nowhere to be found – until someone thought of looking in a Palace refrigerator. Despite it all the procession left for the Abbey only one minute late, at 11.16 am.

The Household Cavalry, in full ceremonial dress for the first time since the dark days of war, accompanied the Irish State Coach, which carried the Princess and her father, the King. The Queen and Princess Margaret were up ahead in the Glass Coach. In between, in her stately Rolls-Royce, came Queen Mary, who delighted the crowds by switching on her interior light so they could see her through the November gloom.

Last into the Abbey, only just before the bride herself, was Winston Churchill, never one to miss the chance for a grand entry. The King told his daughter later, in a letter: 'I was so proud of you & thrilled at having you so close to me on our long walk' down the aisle. 'But when I handed your hand to the Archbishop I felt that I had lost something very precious. You were so calm & composed during the service & said your words with such conviction.' The Archbishop of Canterbury declared in his address that the service was 'exactly the same as it would be for any cottager who might be married this afternoon in some small country church in a remote village in the dales'.

A wedding breakfast for 150 people, modest by royal standards, followed the triumphant procession back to the Palace. By late afternoon Princess Margaret and the other bridesmaids and well-wishers were throwing rose petals over the young couple, as they left by open carriage to catch the train which would take them for a brief and modest honeymoon at Broadlands, Earl Mountbatten's country home. With them went the bride's favourite corgi, Susan. That night, the King wrote to his daughter:

> I can, I know, always count on you, & now Philip, to help us in our work. Your leaving us has left a great blank in our lives but do remember that your old home is still yours & do come back to it as much & as often as possible. I can see that you are sublimely happy with Philip, which is right, but don't forget us is the wish of
>
> Your ever loving & devoted
> PAPA

The King had insisted that no photographers were to be permitted beyond the organ screen of the Abbey – a stark contrast, just a generation ago, to the media event which will take place in St Paul's Cathedral on 29 July. The wedding of the Prince of Wales to Lady Diana Spencer will be seen on live television by some 500 million people all over the world (including the Eastern bloc). It has even been suggested that St Paul's was chosen over Westminster Abbey, the more traditional setting, because the sight-lines are better for television and still cameras. The Royal Family, to be sure, were not dismayed by that particular bonus when they discussed outline arrangements with the BBC's royal liaison man, Cliff Morgan (who also advised them that the end of July would be an ideal time, as it would not clash with other major outside broadcasts such as the Wimbledon tennis championships and the British Open Golf tournament). 'It will be beautiful, glamorous and exciting,' said Mr Morgan, 'the most important and biggest event we have covered since the Coronation of 1936. That's not being sycophantic. It's what the people love.'

But there were two other reasons for the choice of St Paul's, which was an entirely independent decision made by the Prince and Lady Diana themselves. The first, as is well known, is that they wanted to accommodate as many guests as possible, and St Paul's has the larger capacity: 10,000 people crowded in for the service celebrating the end of the Second World War, but as many as 3,000 can be seated comfortably for a major occasion such as this. The other, less well-known reason is that Westminster Abbey holds recent, painful associations for both bride and groom. It was in the Abbey in 1954 that Lady Diana's parents were married, in one of the society weddings of the year – only to separate when the future Princess was just six years old, and to divorce two years later. And it was in the Abbey, only two summers ago, that Prince Charles attended the funeral service of his favourite uncle, Lord Mountbatten, after his murder at the hands of IRA terrorists. St Paul's, by contrast, has such happier recent associations as the thanksgiving services for the Queen's Silver Jubilee in 1977, and for the Queen Mother's eightieth birthday in 1980.

When the announcement was made, on 3 March, the staff at Westminster Abbey were naturally dismayed. 'We are very disappointed. We had been hoping it would come to us,' said the Dean of Westminster, the Very Reverend Dr Edward Carpenter. 'But it was a personal decision of the Prince and Lady Diana. We wish them every happiness. Good luck to the Prince of Wales.' Over at St Paul's, free of scaffolding for the first time in eight years after a £2.5 million restoration appeal, his counterpart, the Very Reverend Alan Webster, positively bubbled with delight. 'It is our intention that St Paul's should be looking its best, with flowers, banners and glorious music,' he said. 'We hope too that the procession to St Paul's up Ludgate Hill will be a wonderful sight.'

It was certainly all hands on deck the last time a Prince of Wales was married at St Paul's – on 14 November (coincidentally enough, Prince Charles's birthday) 1501, when the sickly Arthur, Prince of Wales, was married in the early morning to the Princess Catherine of Aragon. In the absence of her father, King Ferdinand of Spain, the bride was conducted to the altar by the groom's younger brother, ten-year-old Prince Henry – who eight years later was to marry her himself. The old cathedral was destroyed a century and a half later in the Great Fire of London.

Princely weddings have taken place in the early morning, late at night, in sundry different settings around London and Windsor. The last wedding of a Prince of Wales, that of Bertie to Alexandra in 1863, was celebrated in fairly modest style at St George's Chapel, Windsor, because of the recent death of Albert, the Prince Consort; the groom's mother, Queen Victoria, watched in widow's weeds from a discreet balcony named Queen Catherine of Aragon's Closet. Though few, least of all the bbc's main commentator, Tom Fleming, will be rash enough to draw any regal comparisons, the ghost of Catherine, it seems, will at moments hover over the events of 29 July.

The wedding will be the first at the high altar of St Paul's in some time; John Harrison, the chief clerk of the Archbishop of Canterbury's faculty office, said he could remember only one in the last twenty-five years, that of the daughter of the then Bishop of London, Dr Stopford. The Dean of St Paul's has said he plans 'a holy and homely feeling amid the grandeur – a village wedding in the presence of millions of viewers through television.' That 'homely feeling' will also be relayed by close-circuit tv to an overflow audience in the Cathedral crypt.

Television, indeed, was one of the first items on the agenda when planning began only five short months before the event. The bbc, who envisage seven full hours of coverage, costing £150,000 – at £21,000 per hour, a mere two-thirds the cost of an average hour of bbc television – are budgeting for the use of sixty outside broadcast cameras, twelve of them in the Cathedral itself, involving twelve mobile control rooms and some 300 personnel. bbc and itv negotiators have agreed to toss a coin for several tight camera positions within the Cathedral.

A chain of organizational committees for the whole event has been set up under the general supervision of the Lord Chamberlain, Lord Maclean, aged sixty-four, a Justice of the Peace and former Guards officer with broad experience of royal ceremonial. Extra staff have been taken on in his cramped office in St James's Palace, and a helping hand has been lent by the country's senior Duke, the Duke of Norfolk, who carries the hereditary title of Earl Marshal and Chief Butler of England. The wedding, said the editor of Debrett's, would be 'the last great state event of this century'. Lord Maclean entered into the spirit of the thing with his first decree, which was to ease the usual restrictions on the use of the royal crests, insignia and faces in the manufacture of souvenirs to mark the occasion.

The Lord Chamberlain's committees have as a recent precedent for their plans the wedding of Princess Anne to Captain Mark Phillips in 1973, on 14 November (Prince Charles's twenty-fifth birthday). Like many recent royal weddings, it took place at a time of economic and industrial crisis, the seemingly perennial 'winter of discontent' which led to the State of Emergency, the three-day week and the fall of the Heath Government after its confrontation with the miners. The day before the wedding, 'unlucky 13 November', a series of stringent crisis measures had been announced. But as usual, the political climate did nothing to dampen public ardour on the big day itself.

It was clear from the arrival in London of more than 200 foreign journalists that royal nuptials had entered the era of modern satellite communications; Anne's wedding was going to dazzle the entire world even more than had her aunt's to Antony Armstrong-Jones thirteen years before. For the first time in the modern era of royal weddings, security was a predominant issue. Plain-clothed Special Branch men were among the thousands who slept the bitterly cold night on the pavements along the parade route, and mingled with the crowd next morning; the day passed without incident, but less than six months later there was to be an armed kidnap attempt against the Princess and her husband as they drove down the Mall.

Anne decided to dispense with several royal traditions, the first (and to her most significant) being the appointment of her own, then comparatively un-known, dress designer, Maureen Baker of Susan Small Ltd, to design her wedding gown. 'I was certain', said Baker in a state of delighted shock, 'that the dress would go to somebody like Hartnell.' In much the same way, emphasizing her commitment to the fashions of her own generation, Lady Diana Spencer has commissioned a fashionable young husband-and-wife team, David and Eliza-beth Emanuel, whose clothes have been worn by such disparate luminaries as Princess Michael of Kent, the actress Susan Hampshire, the singer Lulu, and the exotic Bianca Jagger. The Emanuels, early in March, were responsible for the dramatic black, strapless taffeta evening gown which caused such a sensation when worn by Lady Diana on her first public outing with Prince Charles after the announcement of their engagement.

David and Elizabeth Emanuel opened their Brook Street business only four years ago, after both had graduated from the Royal College of Art. They worked originally for major stores, their clothes being snapped up by Harrods in London and Neiman-Marcus in the United States. But business got 'too good'; they were expanding so fast they would have had to employ a design manager – 'and we didn't', said David, 'want to do that.' So they turned their attentions to one-of-a-kind couture dresses, for which they were soon attracting an array of illustrious clients, including several of the younger female Royals. The price of Diana's wedding dress is as much an unmentionable as its design. 'It may be the dress of the century,' said David Emanuel, 'but it will also be the secret of the century.'

Princess Anne, in 1973, also broke with tradition by having the Army Catering Corps bake her wedding cake – a privilege usually reserved on royal occasions for the Queen's caterers, Lyons, or Macvitie and Price Ltd. As tall as the Princess herself, the cake was made in four tiers and weighed 145 lbs. Her decision was, in fact, more by way of a public relations move, as there had been considerable public outcry about an Army 'whip-round' for a wedding present for the couple.

The two other precedents set by Anne are not so easy for her elder brother, the heir apparent, to follow. She dispensed with the usual array of bridal attendants, saying that her own copious experience as a bridesmaid had taught her 'what it's like to have yards of uncontrollable children'. She opted for just two miniature escorts: her cousin Sarah, the then nine-year-old daughter of the Earl and Countess of Snowdon, and her nine-year-old brother Edward, who donned the kilt for the occasion.

Anne, moreover, in an attempt to scale down the occasion to 'manageable' proportions, drastically cut back the number of foreign dignitaries invited. Heads of state and reigning monarchs were, to the consternation of many, not on the invitation list. (The one exception, for reasons never explained, was Prince Rainier of Monaco, whose wife, Princess Grace, shocked the fashion commentators by arriving at the Abbey in conspicuous white. 'It just isn't done', shrilled one the next day, 'for anyone but the bride to wear white.' Sniffed another: 'Outrageous'.)

For the wedding of the future King and Queen of Britain, there can be few such relaxations of the royal rules. Royalty, heads of state and politicians from all over the world have been invited, and most will endeavour to attend. (The Deputy Assistant Commissioner of the Metropolitan Police, forty-six-year-old John Radley, head of the London constabulary's uniformed branch, was soon after the announcement of the engagement deputed to organize protection of

all visiting foreign dignitaries.) There are also unlikely to be any snubs such as
that made to Prince Philip's sisters before his own wedding in 1947: they had
all married Germans, and they were all, so soon after the war, left off the guest
list. The only hiccup as yet recorded in the 1981 arrangements, which may
never have reached the ears of Buckingham Palace, took place in Washington,
where it required all the powers of the White House protocol staff to explain to
the forward new First Lady, Mrs Nancy Reagan, that she could not expect to
be seated in the front pew at St Paul's.

Prince Charles's one break with tradition – announced by Buckingham
Palace on 1 April, when he was safely out of the country touring New Zealand
– is that he will have no best man. The elder of his two younger brothers, Prince
Andrew, second only to Charles in line of succession to the throne, was confi-
dently expected to be the obvious choice. Instead Charles – who has decided to
be married in full-dress naval uniform – will have *two* 'supporters': Prince
Andrew and their younger brother Prince Edward. Edward, merely a pageboy
at his sister Anne's wedding eight years ago, will thus undertake his first major
public engagement at Charles's wedding. To satisfy his wounded pride, Prince
Andrew will enjoy the traditional best man's duty of handing over the wedding
ring – which will be struck, as is traditional, from a vein of gold in the Welsh
mountains.

For the Earl Spencer, who will, of course, conduct his daughter down the
aisle to 'give her away', the occasion has one unique and especial delight: for
once, the father of the bride doesn't have to foot the cost of the wedding. As it
happens, despite the murmurings of Willie Hamilton MP and assorted Labour
councillors around the country, the cost to the British taxpayer will not be
extensive. Shared between the St Paul's authorities, and the Ministries of
Environment, Defence and the Home Office, will be the cost of police overtime,
of stands specially constructed along the parade route, and such incidentals as
the transportation of troops to and from the scene, and the clearing-up after-
wards. The brunt of the cost will be borne by the Queen herself, with no extra
allowance being made for the occasion from the Civil List. After Princess Anne's
wedding, the Queen personally signed cheques covering the cost of her daughter's trousseau, the wedding gown, the printing of the invitations, the cake, the
flowers in the Abbey, and other such familiar wedding expenses. She will be
doing the same again in 1981.

By nightfall on 29 July, the newlyweds' family and friends will be waving
them off to a honeymoon on the royal yacht, HMS *Britannia*, in the Caribbean.
Charles and Diana will go through all the usual 'happy couple' embarrassments
– confetti, old boots and practical jokes of the kind which so appeal to the Royal

Family – but they will at least be spared the fate meted out to many of their forebears: the 'Bedding of the Princess', a cherished ritual even in Hanoverian times. When Frederick Louis, Prince of Wales, married Augusta of Saxe-Gotha in 1736, the wedding night was far from private. In Dulcie M. Ashdown's account:

> Augusta was released from the agonies of her stays and put into an ornate nightgown by the Queen herself, then led to her bed. In nightshirt and lace cap ('a grenadier's bonnet', scoffed his mother), Frederick joined her. Side by side they sat while the Court streamed by them, avid to lose no detail of the scene. Then candles were dowsed and Frederick and Augusta, Prince and Princess of Wales, were left alone.

In mediaeval times, the public celebration of a royal wedding often lasted a week or more. This royal wedding, unlike that of Princess Anne, has been declared a one-day national public holiday. But it is only in recent years that the people at large have again been invited to share – if not quite 'take part' – in such occasions. Until the time of Victoria, royal weddings were essentially private celebrations, conducted far from the public gaze, and often far from cheerfully. If the bride and groom were marked down for each other from birth, or had never met, or couldn't stand the sight of each other, there didn't seem much point in asking the nation to share the general mood of indifference.

In our own century, royal matches have at last become occasions, once again, for public rejoicing. Charles and Diana are the symbol of the monarchy's attempts to catch up with the times, and to square up to the challenges of the twenty-first century. Charles is perhaps the first heir apparent in British history to have had such freedom of choice in his quest for a bride; with his mother, he is certainly one of the few who have been able to let his head and his heart have equal say in the decision. It is thus appropriate that, through the technological wizardry of contemporary communications, more people will 'attend' his wedding in St Paul's than have ever attended any wedding in the history of the plighting of troths.

CHAPTER EIGHT

Happily Ever After

'**G**RAND news this morning about the engagement,' said a female civil servant in Lancashire. 'Of course it had been expected for some time, but it seems no less exciting when it is officially announced. I should like to have been among the crowd in the Mall this evening ...' The announcement, said another woman, was 'one of those pleasant and happy events which no one can object to, and which the British people invariably love.' Even four months before the wedding, it was hard not to know that it was happening; a poll of 112 people in London found only one, a road-sweeper in Bloomsbury, who confessed total ignorance. 'Feel? What should I feel?' ... 'I don't care, it doesn't affect me' ... and 'It's not my business. It's up to them' were other less typical comments. Said a less-well-off woman aged thirty: 'I think it's a damned waste of money. I don't see why she should have everything when there are so many who have to make do with makeshift weddings, and others who can't get married at all because they have no homes to go to.'

The 'she' was not Lady Diana Spencer, but Princess Elizabeth, whose engagement to Prince Philip of Greece and Denmark, the newly renamed Lieutenant Philip Mountbatten RN, had just been announced in the summer of 1947. It was a time when the country was recovering from a debilitating war, a time of great privation and hardship for the British people – but a time, for all that, not wholly incomparable with the summer of 1981, when many sections of British society have been brought to their knees by the harsh, unforgiving economic policies of Mrs Margaret Thatcher's Conservative Government.

In 1947, the Camden Town First Branch of the Amalgamated Society of Woodworkers sent the King a stern letter:

> ... to remind you that any banqueting and display of wealth will be an insult to the British people at the present time. Furthermore, should you declare the wedding day a public holiday, you will have a word beforehand with the London Master Builders Association to ensure that we are paid for it.

Between the announcement in July and the wedding in November, however, the proportion of people who actively approved of the celebrations rose from forty to sixty per cent. A fortnight before the ceremony, the percentage of those who still felt the arrangements to be too lavish had fallen to twenty-nine. 'It would have been astonishing', writes Philip Ziegler in his study of the monarchy, *Crown and People* (1978), 'if the proportion had not been dramatically smaller on the day itself.'

Ziegler's work is based in part on the Mass Observation Archive at Sussex University, the remarkable collection of views on matters of the day recorded since 1937 by people at all levels of British society. From Mass Observation's records, Ziegler compiles a portrait of the 1947 wedding day which will surely find echoes in 1981:

> ... It proved hard indeed to remain remote from the proceedings. In a typical provincial office all talk was of the Royal Family. A wireless set was put on upstairs: 'We couldn't get into the room and just joined the crowd clustered outside the room.' In a Scottish factory work stopped almost entirely: 'They may just have been glad of the break,' said a manager dubiously, 'but they certainly *seemed* enthusiastic enough.' Next day a socialist Mass Observer in Manchester tried to buy a newspaper. 'I found every paper sold. I was astonished, but was told the reason was that people wanted to see pictures of the royal wedding. I think there is no doubt that the Royal Family is very popular. Were they to disappear, the people would be very upset.'

In an age before television, when the only access to the wedding outside London was via wireless and the newspapers, the enthusiasm seemed remarkable. 'The feeling is genuine,' wrote a woman from Leatherhead, Surrey, 'a delighted sort of family feeling. I always get it when watching any royal do.' Some just couldn't understand it. 'I think people who slept on pavements in the cold and wet are crazy,' said a housewife in Sheffield, balefully predicting pneumonia for all concerned. In the post-war gloom, many appreciated the fairy-tale glitter of the occasion: 'All of us are hungry for colour, romance and adventure. Today's ceremony symbolizes some sort of dormant form of perfection alive in the breast of every average – well – woman at least.' To others it was the appeal of the Royal Family as a symbol of domestic decency, respectability, solidarity: '... We demand some sort of symbol of what is perhaps, emotionally, the most important part of our way of life – the family.' The most commonly expressed view, interestingly enough, combined fierce patriotism with a degree of chauvinism, almost xenophobia: 'I wonder what foreigners would think of our loyal greetings to the crown,' wrote a male Mass Observer in south-east London. 'I expect that some of the royal visitors would feel jealous, and wonder whether they would get the same kind of greeting in their own countries?' It was a sentiment, as Philip Ziegler concludes, 'that was to grow in stridency over the next twenty-five years.... As the power of Britain waned, so pride grew in the Royal Family as something which was uniquely ours and which no country could match.'

By the time of Elizabeth II's Silver Jubilee in 1977, that sentiment had reached its zenith. A curious species of nationalism, manifested in pride in the Royal Family at every level of a far from classless society, combined with an unusually intoxicating version of the 'any-excuse-for-a-good-time' syndrome. There were 10,000 street parties in London alone, countless thousands more around the country. Neighbours met each other for the first time, and developed lasting friendships. Community spirit was to the fore: 'There's been nothing like this since the Blitz,' was a common sentiment. The parade through London for the thanksgiving service at St Paul's (during which Prince Charles nearly fell off his horse) was another milestone in the recent history of royal media events. There were fireworks over the Thames, a chain of beacons across the country. But the celebrations, in effect, lasted all year, and were merely highlighted by that heady week in midsummer. The popular fervour took everyone by surprise, not least the Queen herself, who echoed her grandfather when she declared, 'I never realized I was loved so much.' Nearly fifty years before, as he rode through London on his Silver Jubilee parade, George V had said to Queen Mary: 'I had no idea they felt like that about me. I'm beginning to think they must really like me for myself.'

Just four years after Elizabeth's Jubilee, this royal wedding will again witness a great national outpouring of respect and affection for the monarchy, a reaffirmation that it approaches the twenty-first century as secure as ever. Elizabeth II believes history will remember her for having rebuilt the institution, on foundations laid by her father, after the abdication crisis of 1936 brought it almost to its knees. Nearly half a century later, as other thrones all over the world have toppled, the British constitutional monarchy is perhaps more stable than at any time in its history.

With that in mind, the wedding will no doubt provoke a further burst of public discussion of the possibility of the Queen's abdicating, at some future point to be determined, in her son's favour. The British people are inordinately fond of their monarch, but they appear to think it cruel and unusual punishment to make the Prince of Wales wait until his dotage to come into his inheritance. The Prince, for instance, will be forty-two when his mother reaches her sixty-fifth birthday; that, it might seem, would be an ideal moment for the Queen to retire to the life of a country lady, and for the nation to crown a new King at the height of his powers.

Early in 1980, when Queen Juliana of the Netherlands abdicated in just such a fashion, in favour of her daughter Beatrix, a Marplan poll conducted for *Now!* magazine revealed an astonishing extent of support for a British abdication. No less than sixty-eight per cent of those sampled were in favour; fifty-eight per cent believed the Queen should hand over 'at a fixed age', with ten per cent urging her to do it 'now', at the age of fifty-three.

The figures did not go down at all well in Buckingham Palace (apart from the reassurance they provided about Prince Charles's public popularity; this was the poll in which, for the first time, he won a higher popularity rating than the Queen herself). Whatever pressures public opinion may bring to bear in the years ahead, Elizabeth II has made a firm decision not to contemplate abdication. The subject, in the Palace, is taboo.

It was not always thus. The very word abdication has sent a collective shudder through Palace circles since 1936, and to some extent still does. But in 1965, at a select dinner party convened to discuss Prince Charles's higher education, the Queen herself raised it with her distinguished guests, who included the Prime Minister (Harold Wilson), the Archbishop of Canterbury, Lord Mountbatten and the monarch's trusted private secretary, Sir Michael Adeane. 'It might be wise', she said, 'to abdicate at a time when Charles could do better.' 'You may be right,' joked her husband gently. 'The doctors will keep you alive so long!'

The subject was discussed no further than that, but the Queen was clearly testing the waters. In the intervening years, however, she has changed. In her

Silver Jubilee year, Elizabeth II was not averse to boasting that she had already been served by seven Prime Ministers (now eight), and intimates had a sudden vision of her wishing to advance to Victorian venerability. 'Parliaments and ministers pass,' Gladstone once said of Victoria, 'but she abides in lifelong duty, and she is to them as the oak in the forest is to the annual harvest in the field.' The older and more experienced a monarch she becomes, the Queen believes, the greater the affection and respect she will command among her people.

Prince Charles agrees with her. He has said on several occasions – the only member of the Royal Family to have put it on the public record – that his mother will not abdicate, and that he would not wish her to. Their mutual dilemma is, in its way, a paradox. There is nothing the Queen would rather do, in due course of time, than retire to her country homes and lead a more tranquil life among her horses and dogs; and she herself is highly aware of the frustrations attending her son's long wait for his birthright. Prince Charles, in turn, regards the prospect stretching ahead of him as a daunting one.

But both are resolved that an abdication would be the beginning of the end of the British monarchy. 'Kingship', as *The Times* recently put it, 'is not a job, but a status.' If the crown were to become a pensionable job like any other, to be tossed lightly aside at the age of sixty-five, it would be irreparably devalued. The British Royal Family, consciously proud of their position at the top of what is left of the royal league table, believe that this has happened in Holland, where it has also created an irresistible precedent. If Charles were to become King at forty-two, would he have to hand on the throne to his own son when he reached sixty-five?

The public opinion in favour of abdication is well-intentioned, but it fails to perceive the nature of the British monarchy's extraordinary appeal to its subjects. Its majesty lies in its antiquity, its prestige and dignity in its continuity and tradition. The Prince will be hailed King at the very moment of his mother's death; the chain of succession, renewed rather than broken by mortality, is in its way a lingering echo of the divine right of Kings. It is also at the very heart of the monarchy's irrational, almost mystical, hold over the imagination of its people. As Walter Bagehot, its great exegesist, wrote of the British constitutional monarchy: 'If you begin to poke about it, you cannot reverence it. Its mystery is its life. We must not let in daylight upon magic.'

Elizabeth II has shrewdly inched the monarchy closer to its people, while preserving the essential gulf between the two – without which it would assuredly soon crumble. 'The popularity of the monarchy', in the words of Lord Blake, the historian, 'has risen even as its political power has diminished. That process has not been accidental.' The Queen is well aware of the subconscious desire of most of her subjects that their Royals still remain on some kind of pedestal: not quite as high as of old, but certainly distant, lofty and in its way untouchable. Abdication would wobble that pedestal. As much as the Queen and her son think a transfer of 'power' a consummation devoutly to be wished, both have set their faces firmly against it.

So Charles will pass many more years as Prince than as King. The longevity of the females of the Houses of Saxe-Coburg-Gotha and Windsor is formidable: Queen Victoria lived to be eighty-one, Queen Mary eighty-five. The present Queen Mother is as old as the century and still going strong. The Prince of Wales, twenty-two years younger than his mother, must expect – and hope – that she will live at least as long. Not for him, however, the attitude of his great-great-grandfather, Bertie, Prince of Wales. 'I don't mind praying to the eternal Father,' Bertie told the Archbishop conducting Victoria's Diamond Jubilee service in 1897, when he was approaching sixty, 'but I must be the only man in the country afflicted with an eternal mother.'

What can Charles make of the job? The ideal monarch, in the gospel according to Bagehot, is one who is 'willing to labour, superior to pleasure and ... begins early to reign.' Bagehot's *The English Constitution* agonized at length over the constitutional role of the Prince of Wales, but finally failed to define one. All he could say by way of apology for Bertie, who was not giving the job a particularly good name, was the now famous incantation:

> All the world and the glory of it, whatever is most attractive, whatever is most seductive, has always been offered to the Prince of Wales of the day, and always will be. It is not rational to expect the best virtue where temptation is applied in the most trying form at the frailest time of human life.

Charles's marriage will, one trusts, deliver him from such temptation. He has already proved himself a very different character from Bertie. But he has, in his agonies over the years ahead, also displayed a deeply sympathetic understanding of the dilemma which faced the last Prince of Wales, his great-uncle, after he had met and decided to marry Mrs Wallis Simpson of Baltimore.

When television's abdication soap opera, *Edward and Mrs Simpson*, was first showing in Britain in 1978, it was Prince Charles who defended his immediate predecessor against the criticism of his own staff, who were levelling such charges as self-indulgence and dereliction of duty. (The argument raged in Buckingham Palace, as in homes throughout the kingdom, all over again.) The two had a fond and thoughtful meeting in October 1970, when Prince Charles dropped by to pay his respects to his exiled uncle during a brief visit to Paris. And it was the Duke of Windsor, the only former Prince of Wales (and King) to have written his own memoirs, who best summed up the frustrations inherent in the job:

> Like the parliamentary system the constitutional monarch who stands aloof from and above politics is a British invention. As a device for preserving the crown as a symbol of national unity while divesting it from abhorrent forms of absolutism, it is a remarkable example of the British genius for accommodation. But one effect of the system, which is perhaps not so well understood by the public, is the handicap imposed on a Prince, who, while obliged to live and work within one of the most intensely political societies on earth, is expected to remain not merely above party and faction, but a-political.

Edward, during his glamorous years as Prince of Wales, exploited the capacity of the office to appeal to the consciences of politicians. Even two nights before his abdication, he was – in the words of his brother, the Duke of York, about to become King George VI *malgré lui* – 'telling the PM [Baldwin] things I am sure he had never heard before about the unemployed centres etc (referring to his visit in S. Wales)'. The Duke whispered to his neighbour at table, Walter Monckton: 'And this is the man we are about to lose....'

But Edward, as King, never quite grasped the constitutional limitations of his office; as Prince, he perhaps overestimated them. He never took the opportunity, for instance, to speak in the House of Lords. King Edward VII, when Prince of Wales, exceeded Bagehot's expectations by speaking in the Lords on many occasions, even on one of them voting in favour of an Act in which his family had a special interest (to legalize marriage with a deceased wife's sister). To his great delight, he was invited to serve on the Royal Commission on the Housing of the Working Classes; he threw himself into it with a will, even donning a disguise to tour the slums of the East End on a personal visit of inspection. In 1879, Bertie attended debates in the Lords on no less than nineteen occasions; Prince Charles has so far spoken there twice.

But Charles faces a particular problem which confronted neither of his immediate predecessors. In her anxiety to avoid what she herself has called an 'Edward VII situation', his mother has ensured for some years now that he receives his own 'boxes', the battered maroon attaché cases containing state and Cabinet papers, and that he is able to meet and converse with politicians on a Privy Council basis – that is, in total confidentiality. He must, nevertheless, always avoid taking any party political position, and must be very careful when opening his mouth on any subject that may loosely be construed as political. While uniquely well-informed on the minutiae of day-to-day government business, therefore, Prince Charles must continually bite his tongue on subjects close to his heart.

When he crosses the sacred divide, as he has on occasion quite deliberately, unholy rows ensue. In July 1978, when Pope Paul VI refused a church wedding to his cousin, Prince Michael of Kent, because his bride-to-be was a divorcée, the Prince of Wales made a fighting speech condemning the Churches for causing 'needless distress' with their continuing doctrinal disputes. He was denounced by the Vatican for 'sheer impertinence', and there followed two weeks of letters to *The Times* under the gratifying headline 'The Prince and the Pope'. Charles was delighted; his parents were not. When he returned to London from an official visit to Norway, he was summoned straight home for a carpeting. His father, who can on occasion behave with considerable severity towards the Prince, even now that he is in his thirties, gave him a stern dressing-down. Prince Charles, as always in such circumstances, did not fight back; he took the rebuke very meekly, and spent the next few days in abject misery.

But that, mercifully enough, is the full extent of Prince Charles's disagreements with his parents. He has very few differences of opinion with his mother, whom he deeply resembles in character (Princess Anne taking after the Mountbatten side of the family). There is, of course, a long history of bitterness and conflict between Princes of Wales and their parents, which reached its climax during the Hanoverian family wars, each successive King trying to curb the political power of – and thus the political threat from – his son and heir. None ever went quite as far as Peter the Great, who executed his heir; but George I tried to have his son arrested, and George II ensured that the family tradition was preserved. With the passing of the monarchy's political power, so these political disputes largely died away, though they were echoed in Victoria's insistence that her son, Bertie, be kept well away from the political process. Bertie, as a result, developed the role of the Prince of Wales in British society which we see today.

It is easy to forget that when Bertie went busily about his social duties – opening housing estates, new town halls, agricultural shows – he was doing things that would have been unthinkable for any Prince of Wales before him. In the tradition of Frederick Louis, the unhappily short-lived early eighteenth-century Prince, Bertie held glittering sway over London society, maintaining the monarchy's surface glamour and social influence while his mother moped away at Windsor and Balmoral. But he also fashioned the contemporary monarchy's responsibility for taking a personal interest in its subjects' welfare, by moving among them on frequent occasions and patronizing many of the leading social and welfare organizations. It was Bertie, to be sure, who forged and cemented the British monarchy's remarkably strong bond with the working classes.

He also developed the Prince of Wales's now familiar role as a roving am-
bassador-without-portfolio overseas – thanks to his mother's dislike of travel
and his own inordinate enthusiasm for it. And he continued, meanwhile, the
distinguished tradition whereby the Prince of Wales uses his office as a unique
opportunity to support and patronize the arts. Charles I, one of the most
accomplished of all English Kings, developed his aesthetic tastes and interests
while Prince of Wales; it is the one area where the Hanoverian Princes, notably
Frederick Louis and the Prince Regent, distinguished themselves.

Prince Charles, as we have seen, is intent on maintaining these traditions. In
the field of the arts, particularly, he has already shown more genuine interest
and expertise than might be expected of his genes, and has used his position to
its very best advantage in his considerable work for the Royal Opera House,
Covent Garden. But the world, as the Cambridge historian J.H. Plumb has
written, 'has greatly changed since Edward VII gave new directions to the role
of Prince of Wales. . . . Perhaps the time has come for further innovation. If so,
that must come, as it did with Edward VII, from inner conviction, not from
advice.'

Plumb, like so many before him, did not go on to put forward any specific
suggestions. They are not easy to come up with. Prince Charles himself has said
that he wants 'to change the old, remote image of royalty', and has also
declared: 'In these times, this sort of organization is called into question. It is
not taken for granted as it used to be. In that sense one has to be far more
professional than I think one ever used to be.' He has publicly acknowledged
that late twentieth-century Britain is 'a really rather minor state', and has
defined his role primarily as 'a form of leadership . . . to help push people along,
to encourage them; to warn, advise, amuse . . . and generally be seen to show an
interest.'

Hitherto he has sought strenuously to establish himself a worthy reputation
among his future subjects, fighting against a tide of playboy-style publicity, and
has already achieved much that is admirable: his social work, his tours of British
government and industry, his trips abroad as an unofficial trade ambassador,
his increasing efforts to assume the guardianship of the national morale. Now
his marriage will be an opportunity for innovation, for a conscious reshaping
of his popular image, for 'inventing' a job that he can be seen to be doing. The
answer, surely, lies in British industry.

The Queen's Award for Exports has been one of the most successful royal
innovations of recent years, demonstrating the monarchy's concern to encourage and reward British endeavour in world markets. Once the Prince of Wales's
family life is established, and he has perhaps enjoyed a stint as the Queen's

representative in a Commonwealth country, it would be a shrewd and popular move for him to take an active, even full-time, role in British economic life. There can be no question of his endorsing any one company by joining its board, or lending his name to its notepaper, but there is no reason why he should not head an autonomous, non-governmental body working on industry's behalf. Or even start his own company.

In my previous book, *Charles, Prince of Wales*, I recorded the royal reaction to a thirtieth-birthday suggestion that he found a company called 'HRH Electronics'. It was a time when Britain was dragging its feet in the electronics markets of the world, when British scientists had joined the 'brain drain' to the United States and elsewhere to develop the silicon chip and other such innovations likely to revolutionize modern technology. A royally-sponsored company could pioneer other exemplary innovations, such as worker participation in management and profit-sharing; it would help the monarchy demonstrate publicly that its state subsidy is more than cost-effective; profits could be given to charity or, more realistically, ploughed back into the company; above all, it would give the Prince of Wales a clearly identified and dynamic role of his own. It would give him what most people thought he didn't have: a job. His two younger brothers could take over some of the ritualistic public duties of royalty for which he would be less free. What about it? Wasn't it time the monarchy dropped its inhibitions and rolled up its sleeves?

Not at all, according to the Palace. The notion was described by the Prince as 'tendentious', and got a stern thumbs-down from his then newly appointed private secretary, Edward Adeane. The twentieth-century monarchy, it seemed, was not about to lend its name and ancient dignities to the commercial market. Still less would the family business, whose assets, investments and other finances remain a closely guarded secret, ever 'go public'.

HRH Electronics may be a less than perfect model, but it would be an immensely popular and constructive move if the Prince of Wales and his advisers could come up with some acceptable formula for his greater involvement in British commercial life. There was a similarly blank response from the Palace early in 1981, when a competition in the *Observer* came up with several such suggestions. First prize was awarded to Mr Richard Rowntree, of the Joseph Rowntree Social Service Trust, who proposed that the Prince should serve as chairman of a newly created Co-Operation Development Bank of Wales, which 'would aim to combine full banking services throughout the principality with the provision of loan capital and financial and commercial expertise for the development of industrial co-operative enterprises.'

The remarkable response to the paper's competition – its instigators, Alan

Road and Robin Lustig, were overwhelmed by readers' letters – should demonstrate to the Palace the public concern that the Prince should develop some such active position for himself. The years ahead seem likely to continue the recent trends of social decay in Britain, and the monarchy's greatest service in these straitened times would be to join the fray, to lead the programme for national revival. It would also, most probably, prove a great deal more effective in rallying the national spirit than have our recent political leaders. It will fall to Prince Charles to steward the ancient, irrational institution of monarchy into not merely a new century, but a new millennium; his task will be greatly eased if he has by then developed for himself a specific function, albeit a symbolic one, that suits the times. It would, to be sure, be in character. There is, as was said of the last Prince of Wales, 'no doubt of the young man's capacity for goodness'.

As for his Princess, she must in the early years select a few social and charitable organizations, and make them her own. Princess Anne's work in these areas is underestimated, as is Princess Margaret's. Both have devoted much of their time to the kind of 'volunteer work' of which royalty can prove a uniquely inspiring figurehead – and a great boost to fundraising. It will be important that Diana develop interests independent from those of her husband.

But this Princess, it seems possible, could also in time take over the Prince of Wales's now traditional role as a leader of fashion. Unlike the last two Princes of Wales, Charles has so far displayed little interest in sartorial distinction, which has naturally been a great disappointment to British tailors. Princes of Wales have always been good for business. The Duke of Windsor often wondered, he said, whether 'to certain sections of the press, I was not more of a glorified clothes-peg than the heir apparent'. Over dinner one night at La Croe, near Antibes, he happened to wear a tartan suit of the kind his father, King George v, had been wearing in private for fifty years.

> One of our guests mentioned the fact to a friend in the men's fashion trade, who immediately cabled the news to America. Within a few months tartan had become a popular material for every sort of masculine garment, from dinner jackets and cummerbunds to swimming trunks and beach shorts.

The *Tailor and Cutter* offered moral encouragement to Prince Charles early on, by voting him one of the World's Top Ten Best Dressed Men at the age of four; twenty years later, having received little return on its investment, it denounced his 'cult of studied shabbiness'. The Prince was not perturbed, and continued to wear the tidy, but scarcely dashing, middle-aged clothes which have become his hallmark. His tailor is especially annoyed by the Prince's adamant refusal to wear braces, which results in his trousers hanging baggily around his heels. Lady Diana, by contrast, already has a reputation as something of a fashion plate.

The style-spotters of Fleet Street excelled themselves on discovering a new prey in Lady Di, reading 'vivid imagination' into her colour schemes and everything from 'a daring boldness' to 'demure respectability' into her necklines. Every outfit was analysed in meticulous detail. It was revealed that she would have to wear 'flatties', to avoid appearing taller than her husband; there was an earnest debate over what she might have purchased at the Knightsbridge salon of Janet Reger, purveyor of slinky underwear to the wealthy. From all the mush, it seemed to emerge that Diana combines sensible shopping-around at the 'better' chain stores with the occasional, innovative adornment. Michael Roberts of the *Sunday Times* referred somewhat cruelly to 'the young Margaret Thatcher look', then got carried away in a crescendo of adjectives:

> Gamine and squeaky clean with the sturdy calves of the dedicated cyclist, she doesn't have much – if any – truck with the frills and furbelows of *haute couture* dressing which enthrals such racy royals as Princess Caroline of Monaco (a Dior disciple) or choose a style that's draggy-plus (Princess Marie-Astrid of Luxembourg's Victorian nightie look, for instance).

Within days of the engagement announcement, the 'Lady Di look' was all the rage at hairdressers around the land. Once the Emanuels had been chosen to design her wedding dress, Ellis Bridals of London announced that replicas – hastily copied from television coverage of the ceremony – would be on sale 'within hours' of her walking up the aisle. If the future Queen continues, as seems entirely probable, to appear in public in off-the-peg styles from the major stores, it is no exaggeration to say that she will be making her first important and well-judged contribution to British public life. Not merely would it provide a much-needed boost to both stores and designers, it would indicate a welcome lack of ostentation in these dire economic times. The only difference for Diana will be that instead of nipping round the stores herself, she will have to ask the stores to nip round to her.

'The apparel oft proclaims the man': the Princess of Wales may in time prove herself a more independent and innovative spirit than her husband. She certainly brings to his life a freshness and vitality it had begun to lack – a chance to escape from the claustrophobic corridors of Buckingham Palace, from the benign but restraining influence of his parents, to develop a public style and persona more his own. Hitherto, he has tended to take physical risks more than intellectual ones. One of the results, to his dismay, is that his future subjects regard him as a swashbuckling, outdoor, hairy-chested type rather than the hesitant, kindly, rather vulnerable man he really is. The popular imagination, up to now, has him invariably seated astride a racehorse or a polo pony, where he in fact spends very little of his time, rather than stuck behind his desk, where he spends a great deal. There are two very twentieth-century ironies in the story of Charles's life so far: that the most publicized Prince in history has been among the most misunderstood, and that the many agonized, often bold initiatives taken on his behalf throughout his upbringing have combined to produce the most conventional young Prince of Wales of modern times.

The years ahead, for the Prince and Princess, are in their way enviable: a glamorous and privileged annual round of Klosters and Deauville, Iceland and the Caribbean, Sandringham winters, Balmoral summers, Windsor weekends. The makings of a junior court, to preside over British society, an invitation to which will be the most sought-after in the land. The freedom to move at will among the great, the mighty, the talented, the merely famous. Independence from all the day-to-day practical anxieties which afflict the rest of humankind.

And yet they are not so enviable: the surrender of privacy, of the power of independent decision-making, of – to a considerable extent – personal identity. The trivial round, the common task which is the lot of contemporary royalty. The inability to move freely around the streets of the world, to be an unknown spectator of events, to act on a whim. The loss of spontaneity. The absence of the unexpected. The lack of those liberties which enrich the rest of humankind.

After an already action-packed life, the Prince of Wales now crosses a threshold away from his youth, into a period of increasing challenge. There is time ahead, in abundance, for him to demonstrate as Prince and as King that he can modify both roles, to fit the times, rather than allow them to modify him. He has already displayed a degree of conscientiousness greater than that of many of his predecessors, coupled with deep-seated good intents enough to win him enormous popularity. It is a fitting tribute to this idealistic young Prince that his future subjects now hope he and his bride will live, well, yes, happily ever after.

Prince Charles's Descent

The Royal House of Windsor

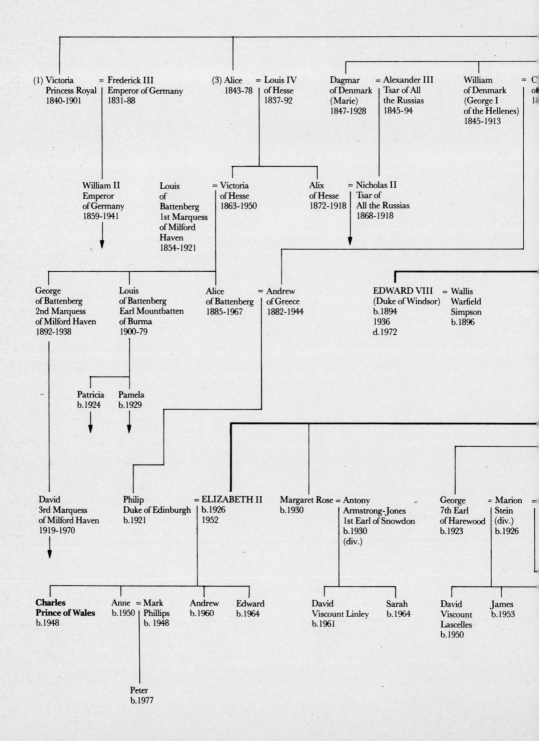

(1) Victoria
Princess Royal
1840-1901

= Frederick III
Emperor of Germany
1831-88

(3) Alice
1843-78

= Louis IV
of Hesse
1837-92

Dagmar
of Denmark
(Marie)
1847-1928

= Alexander III
Tsar of All
the Russias
1845-94

William
of Denmark
(George I
of the Hellenes)
1845-1913

= C
o
1

William II
Emperor
of Germany
1859-1941

Louis
of
Battenberg
1st Marquess
of Milford
Haven
1854-1921

= Victoria
of Hesse
1863-1950

Alix
of Hesse
1872-1918

= Nicholas II
Tsar of
All the Russias
1868-1918

George
of Battenberg
2nd Marquess
of Milford Haven
1892-1938

Louis
of Battenberg
Earl Mountbatten
of Burma
1900-79

Alice
of Battenberg
1885-1967

= Andrew
of Greece
1882-1944

EDWARD VIII
(Duke of Windsor)
b.1894
1936
d.1972

= Wallis
Warfield
Simpson
b.1896

Patricia
b.1924

Pamela
b.1929

David
3rd Marquess
of Milford Haven
1919-1970

Philip
Duke of Edinburgh
b.1921

= ELIZABETH II
b.1926
1952

Margaret Rose
b.1930

= Antony
Armstrong-Jones
1st Earl of Snowdon
b.1930
(div.)

George
7th Earl
of Harewood
b.1923

= Marion
Stein
(div.)
b.1926

=

**Charles
Prince of Wales**
b.1948

Anne
b.1950

= Mark
Phillips
b. 1948

Andrew
b.1960

Edward
b.1964

David
Viscount Linley
b.1961

Sarah
b.1964

David
Viscount
Lascelles
b.1950

James
b.1953

Peter
b.1977

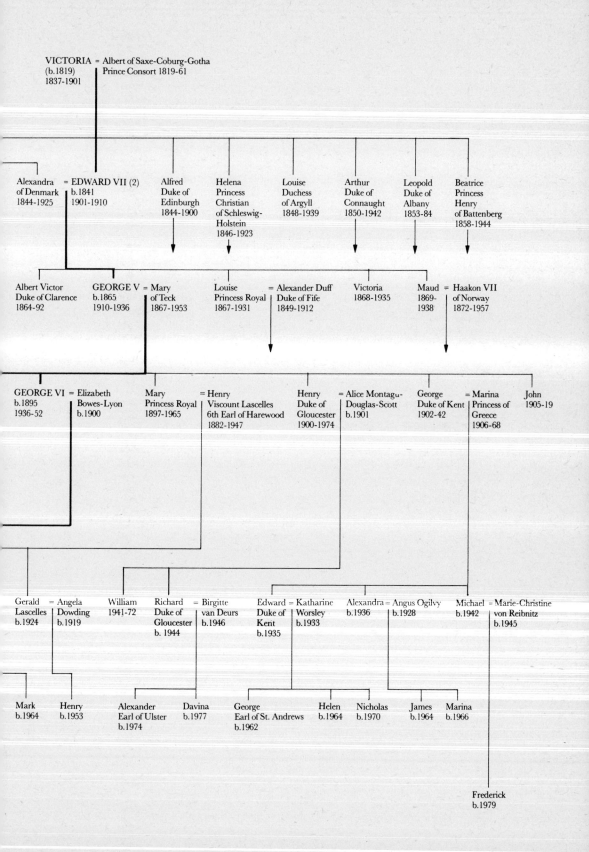

VICTORIA = Albert of Saxe-Coburg-Gotha
(b.1819)   Prince Consort 1819-61
1837-1901

Alexandra   = EDWARD VII (2)   Alfred   Helena   Louise   Arthur   Leopold   Beatrice
of Denmark   b.1841   Duke of   Princess   Duchess   Duke of   Duke of   Princess
1844-1925   1901-1910   Edinburgh   Christian   of Argyll   Connaught   Albany   Henry
                                     1844-1900   of Schleswig-   1848-1939   1850-1942   1853-84   of Battenberg
                                                     Holstein   1858-1944
                                                     1846-1923

Albert Victor   GEORGE V = Mary   Louise   = Alexander Duff   Victoria   Maud = Haakon VII
Duke of Clarence b.1865   of Teck   Princess Royal Duke of Fife   1868-1935   1869-   of Norway
1864-92   1910-1936 1867-1953 1867-1931   1849-1912   1938   1872-1957

GEORGE VI = Elizabeth   Mary   = Henry   Henry   = Alice Montagu-   George   = Marina   John
b.1895   Bowes-Lyon   Princess Royal Viscount Lascelles Duke of   Douglas-Scott   Duke of Kent   Princess of   1905-19
1936-52   b.1900   1897-1965   6th Earl of Harewood Gloucester   b.1901   1902-42   Greece
                                         1882-1947   1900-1974   1906-68

Gerald   = Angela   William   Richard   = Birgitte   Edward = Katharine   Alexandra = Angus Ogilvy   Michael = Marie-Christine
Lascelles   Dowding   1941-72   Duke of   van Deurs   Duke of Worsley   b.1936   b.1928   b.1942   von Reibnitz
b.1924   b.1919   Gloucester   b.1946   Kent   b.1933   b.1945
                                   b. 1944   b.1935

Mark   Henry   Alexander   Davina   George   Helen   Nicholas   James   Marina
b.1964   b.1953   Earl of Ulster   b.1977   Earl of St. Andrews b.1964   b.1970   b.1964   b.1966
                     b.1974   b.1962

Frederick
b.1979

In August 1977, at the age of ninety-two, the late Mr Gerald Paget of Welwyn Garden City, Hertfordshire, published his first book: in two volumes costing £60, containing nearly 1,000 pages and weighing 13 lb., it is entitled *The Lineage and Ancestry of HRH Prince Charles, Prince of Wales*. Mr Paget's introduction opens with the rare and enviable sentence: 'This book had its origin about seventy-five years ago. . . .'

It was in Queen Victoria's Diamond Jubilee year, 1897, that the schoolboy Paget first became interested in genealogy. G. W. Watson's work on the ancestry of King Edward VII, published in *The Genealogist* some ten years later, gave him the idea of tracing the pedigrees of various European monarchs. With the birth of Princess Elizabeth in 1926 he decided to explore her ancestry, hopefully as far as William the Conqueror; but he was still immersed in his project twenty-two years later, when Princess Elizabeth gave birth to Prince Charles. So Paget, then sixty-three, decided to start afresh and pursue the new Prince's ancestry, though the introduction of Prince Philip's lineage of course doubled his work-load. Had he stuck to his original intent, to trace Prince Charles back to William the Conqueror, the theoretical number of ancestors would have risen to the astonishing figure of 1,073,741,824. He decided to call a halt in the fourteenth and fifteenth centuries, at the eighteenth generation. Even so, his monumental publication leaves only some forty thousand ancestors untraced out of a total of 262,142.

These two paragraphs are by way of tribute to Mr Paget's life work, without which this appendix could scarcely have been written. I must also acknowledge a debt to an excellent two-part review of his work, in *Books and Bookmen* (vol. 23, nos 7–8), by the genealogist Sir Iain Moncreiffe of that Ilk, Albany Herald. Sir Iain's voluminous knowledge of his subject was able to detect a few minor errors, and add some intriguing new dimensions; he has also had a large hand in the compilation of this appendix. As he himself says: 'HRH's breeding is the most important in the world . . . he is heir to the world's greatest position that is determined solely by heredity.'

Through cousin marriages many of the ancestors traced by Paget, more than a quarter of a million of them, are of course the same people. The total number of individuals is thus greatly reduced, which is as it should be. The Blood Royal is proportionately the purer.

In Prince Charles's veins runs the blood of emperors and kings, Russian boyars, Spanish grandees, noblemen of every European nation, bishops and judges, knights and squires, and tradesmen right down to a butcher, a toymaker and an innkeeper. Readers curious for more detail than this appendix can provide should turn to Mr Paget's work. His discoveries include the fact that Prince Charles is a cousin or nephew, in varying degrees, of all six wives of Henry VIII; that he has many descents from the Royal Houses of Scotland, France, Germany, Austria, Denmark, Sweden, Norway, Spain, Portugal, Russia and the Netherlands. Many of his ancestors died bloodily, in battle or by the axe, especially in the Wars of the Roses and the reigns of the Tudor sovereigns.

The most significant of Prince Charles's forebears fall into three categories. First there are those who were historic figures in the British Isles, the immediate realm. Secondly, there are similar figures, especially royalty, in the rest of Europe from which emigrants have gone out in such numbers to the Old Commonwealth. And thirdly, there is a leaven of solid British stock of all classes; just enough to keep HRH down to earth, but not enough to dilute his royal blood unduly, or to give him too many inconvenient near-relations among his family's subjects.

In England, he descends over and over again from the Anglo-Saxon, Norman, Plantagenet and Tudor kings, indeed from every English king who has left descendants (even including Henry IV), except Charles I and his sons. He descends from the non-royal Protectors of England, Edward Seymour, Duke of Somerset and John Dudley, Duke of Northumberland (but not from Cromwell; curiously enough, HRH does not take sides genealogically in the Civil War). Other famous characters abound in his ancestry: Alfred the Great; Hereward the Outlaw (better known, incorrectly, as the Wake) hero of the Anglo-Saxon epic, together with the King Harold slain at Hastings *and* their foe William the Conqueror; Simon de Montfort, Earl of Leicester, the first Parliamentarian; Harry 'Hotspur', Lord Percy, hero of the Ballad of Chevy Chase; Warwick the Kingmaker; and the great Elizabethans Essex, the Queen's favourite, Sir Frances Walsingham and William Cecil, Lord Burghley.

Thanks to the lineage of Queen Elizabeth The Queen Mother (born Lady Elizabeth Bowes-Lyon, daughter of the fourteenth Earl of Strathmore), the blood of some of England's noblest houses runs in the Prince of Wales's veins:

including de Vere, Earl of Oxford; Courtenay, Earl of Devon; Percy, Earl of Northumberland; Talbot, Earl of Shrewsbury; Stanley, Earl of Derby; Clifford, Earl of Cumberland; Cecil, Earl of Salisbury; Howard, Duke of Norfolk; Russell, Duke of Bedford, and Cavendish, Duke of Devonshire. Queen Anne's chief minister Robert Harley and the Prime Minister Portland were direct ancestors; Sir Philip Sidney and the 'Iron Duke' of Wellington his ancestral uncles; Charles Darwin, and – through the relationship of the Hastings, Earls of Huntingdon, to the Ardens – probably Shakespeare, were the Prince's ancestral fifth cousins.

In Wales, the present Prince of Wales descends from such renowned characters as Davy Gam and such historic families as Morgan of Tredegar, but above all from the great Owen Glendower (Owain Glyndwr), proclaimed 'Prince of Wales by the Grace of God' during the last Welsh rising. Moreover, he descends many times over from Llewelyn the Great, Prince of Wales, and all Welsh kings and princes by way of Hywel Dda back to Cunedda and Old King Coel himself, who reigned in the fifth century, soon after the Romans left Britain.

In Scotland, the Prince derives his title of Great Steward of Scotland from his ancestors the Stewart kings. Through George VI and Prince Philip he descends *twenty-two times over* from Mary Queen of Scots, and he has more than two hundred direct lines of descent from King Robert Bruce and thus from the ancient Celtic kings of the Picts and Scots. Through the Lyons of Glamis, most of the historic Scottish houses contributed to his lineage: the 'Black Douglas' Earls of Douglas and the 'Red Douglas' Earls of Angus; the 'lightsome' Lindsay Earls of Crawford; the 'handsome' Hay Earls of Errol; the 'gey' (which means ferocious, not gay in any sense) Gordon Earls of Huntly; the 'proud' Graham Earls of Montrose. A rather surprising ancestor was Cardinal Beaton, the murdered Archbishop of St Andrews.

On the Borders his forebears included the Homes of Wedderburn, the 'bold' Scotts of Buccleuch and their foes in many a ballad, the Kerrs of Fernihurst. In the far North, through the first Sinclair Earl of Caithness, he comes from the old Norse jarls of Orkney. In central Scotland, the Prince springs from the Lords Drummond and the Murrays of Tullibardine, the Moncreiffes of that Ilk and Stirlings of Keir, and the Stewart Earls of Atholl. Elsewhere in the Highlands, through his descent from the Grants of Grant and the tenth Chief of Mackintosh, the Prince has Hebridean blood of the mighty Clanranald – and in the West, too, he descends not only from the MacDougall chiefs of Dunollie and the Campbell Earls of Argyll, but above all (as befits the present Lord of the Isles) at least two dozen times over from the paramount Macdonald chiefs who were the original Lords of the Isles.

In Ireland, Queen Elizabeth The Queen Mother has brought Prince Charles the most distinguished Irish ancestry, the blood of the Dal Cais and Eoganacht dynasties of Munster and that of the Ui Neill high kings. Among his ancestors were the O'Brien Earls and Kings of Thomond (including the high kings Brian 'Boru' and Toirdhelbhach); the McCarthy Reagh chieftains of the line of King Cormac who built the famous chapel at Cashel; the O'Donnells of Tyrconnell; the MacDonnells of Antrim (including 'Sorley Boy'); the wild Burkes of Clanricarde; the FitzGerald Earls of Kildare and Desmond, and the Knights of Glin; the Butler Earls of Ormonde; and, above all, Red Hugh O'Neill, Earl of Tyrone, the last native King of Ulster, who died in exile in Rome in 1618.

To turn to the continent of Europe: Prince Charles, through his father, is Danish, in the direct male line of the Royal House of Denmark, which still reigns in Norway. He descends father-to-son through Christian IX, King of Denmark (1863–1906) from Christian I, King of Denmark, Norway and Sweden (1448–81). Among his celebrated Viking ancestors were King Sven Forkbeard of Denmark and King Harold Haardrade of Norway, but he also springs from the ancient 'Peace-Kings', whose vast grave-mounds can still be seen at Uppsala in Sweden. King Canute was his ancestral uncle. So too were Gustavus Adolphus and Charles XII of Sweden, for his Scandinavian ancestry is octopoid, taking in the Royal House of Vasa as well as such locally historic names as Oxenstierna and Sture, Sparre and Gyllenstierna, Baner and Konigsmark, Bonde and Bielke.

In Russia, he is descended through Czar Nicholas I from both Catherine the Great and Peter the Great. He also has innumerable descents from the Grand Princes of the House of Rurik, who originally founded 'All The Russias', among them St Vladimir of Kiev, who Christianized the Russians; Yuri Dolgoruky, celebrated as the founder of Moscow; and St Michael of Chernigov, executed by the Tartars for refusing to kneel to a statue of Genghis Khan. In Poland, he descends from the original Piast dynasty and from the Jagiellons up to King Zygmunt I (died 1548). His Lithuanian ancestry goes back to Gedimin, last pagan sovereign of Lithuania (1316–41). His Byzantine imperial blood flows from the Angeloi and Comnenoi emperors of the East, and through the House of Savoy from the later Emperors Michael VIII and Andronicus Palaeologue.

In Bohemia, the Prince descends from all the kings who have left descendants, from the original Czech house of Premsyl (the family of Good St Wenceslas) down through the House of Luxembourg to Anne of Bohemia, wife of the Emperor Ferdinand I. So his ancestors include the 'Blind King' slain at Crécy, the Emperor Charles IV who founded the University of Prague, and above all the popular Hussite elected King George of Podiebrad. Other historic Czech names in the Prince's ancestry are Lobkowicz and Sternberg, and Ulric 'the lame lord' of Rosenberg. In Hungary, he similarly descends from all the kings (who left issue) of the original Royal House of Arpad; moreover, the famous King John Szapolyai was his ancestral uncle. Also, through his great-grandmother Queen Mary, the blood of many Magyar noble families, including several of the Bathory voivodes of Transylvania, flows in his veins. In Romania, by way of Queen Mary's ancestry, he descends from Vlad Dracul, Voivode of Wallachia (father of the original Dracula) and thus from the Bassarab dynasty who were very possibly derived from Genghis Khan himself.

In what was the Holy Roman Empire, he descends over and over again from Charlemagne and Frederick Barbarossa and all the great dynasties, Habsburg and Hohenstaufen, Guelph and Hohenzollern, Bavaria and Saxony, Hesse and Baden, Mecklenburg and Württemberg, Brunswick and Anhalt, the Electors Palatine and other Wittelsbachs, plus many of the historic houses such as Hohenlohe and Galen, Moltke and Sickingen, Schwarzenberg and Trauttmansdorff. Otto the Great and Phillip of Hesse were his direct forefathers. Frederick the Great and the Emperor Charles v were his ancestral uncles.

In Portugal, the Prince descends from the marriage of the son of King John I of Aviz, Alfonso, Duke of Braganza, to Beatrix, daughter of the Blessed Nuño Alvarez Pereira, the 'Holy Constable'. The equally celebrated infante Henry the Navigator was an ancestral uncle.

In Italy, his forefathers include the Dukes of Savoy and the Emperor Frederick II 'Stupor Mundi' and the mediaeval Kings of Sicily, as also the Orsini of Rome (Pope Nicholas III was his ancestral uncle), the Visconti of Milan, della Scala of Verona, Doria of Genoa and Gonzaga of Mantua (besides the great *condottieri* Colleoni and Hawkwood); in Spain, they include Ferdinand and Isabella (who financed Columbus's discovery of America) and thus El Cid himself. In France the Carolingian, Capetian and Valois kings up to Charles VII (the Dauphin of Joan of Arc fame), among them St Louis many times over, and such historic names as Montmorency and Rohan, Polignac and La Rochefoucauld and La Tour d'Auvergne. In the Netherlands: through his wife Charlotte of Bourbon, none other than William the Silent, Prince of Orange and founder of the Dutch Republic. In the Low Countries, too, Prince Charles bears a remarkable likeness to portraits of Charles the Bold, Duke of Burgundy, who was his direct forefather.

HRH's immemorial roots of course go back far, far beyond the generations covered by Mr Paget's monumental work. The Prince's Anglo-Saxon and Danish royal forefathers sprang from Dark Age kings who incarnated the storm-spirit Woden (after whom Wednesday is named), and among his pagan Celtic royal forefathers were King Niall of the Nine Hostages and the dynamic Iron

Age sacral kings of Tara, the great sanctuary of ancient Ireland. Through the Lusignan crusader kings of Cyprus, titular kings of Jerusalem, Prince Charles descends a millennium further back from King Tiridates the Great, the first Christian monarch of all (under whom Armenia was converted in AD 314, before even Rome itself), and thus from the divine Parthian imperial House of Arsaces (247 BC), which reigned over Persia and Babylonia and was in its time the mightiest dynasty in the Ancient World.

Finally, down to earth. In 1779 Mr George Carpenter, of Redbourn in Hertfordshire (writes Sir Anthony Wagner, Garter King of Arms, in his *English Genealogy*) 'had the plumber down from London to repair the roof of his house. With the plumber came his daughter, and both remained at Redbourn some time. Mary Elizabeth Walsh, the daughter, was then eighteen years of age, and Mr Carpenter upwards of sixty, yet notwithstanding the disparity of their ages and positions he married her. Their daughter married the 11th Earl of Strathmore' – the Queen Mother's great-great-grandfather. The Prince of Wales is thus eighth in descent from that plumber, John Walsh. There are many other plain English names in his ancestry; but it is through the plainest of them all, John Smith, that Prince Charles is one of the nearest living relations of George Washington, first President of the United States.

Lady Diana Spencer's Descent

Lady Diana Spencer's Royal Ancestry

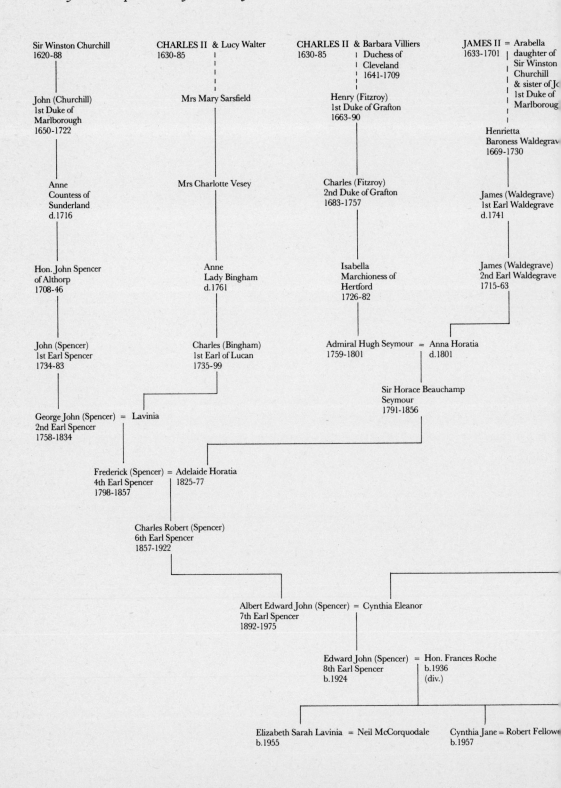

Sir Winston Churchill
1620-88

John (Churchill)
1st Duke of
Marlborough
1650-1722

Anne
Countess of
Sunderland
d.1716

Hon. John Spencer
of Althorp
1708-46

John (Spencer)
1st Earl Spencer
1734-83

CHARLES II & Lucy Walter
1630-85

Mrs Mary Sarsfield

Mrs Charlotte Vesey

Anne
Lady Bingham
d.1761

Charles (Bingham)
1st Earl of Lucan
1735-99

CHARLES II & Barbara Villiers
1630-85   Duchess of
     Cleveland
     1641-1709

Henry (Fitzroy)
1st Duke of Grafton
1663-90

Charles (Fitzroy)
2nd Duke of Grafton
1683-1757

Isabella
Marchioness of
Hertford
1726-82

Admiral Hugh Seymour = Anna Horatia
1759-1801   d.1801

JAMES II = Arabella
1633-1701   daughter of
     Sir Winston
     Churchill
     & sister of Jo
     1st Duke of
     Marlboroug

Henrietta
Baroness Waldegrav
1669-1730

James (Waldegrave)
1st Earl Waldegrave
d.1741

James (Waldegrave)
2nd Earl Waldegrave
1715-63

Sir Horace Beauchamp
Seymour
1791-1856

George John (Spencer) = Lavinia
2nd Earl Spencer
1758-1834

Frederick (Spencer) = Adelaide Horatia
4th Earl Spencer   1825-77
1798-1857

Charles Robert (Spencer)
6th Earl Spencer
1857-1922

Albert Edward John (Spencer) = Cynthia Eleanor
7th Earl Spencer
1892-1975

Edward John (Spencer) = Hon. Frances Roche
8th Earl Spencer   b.1936
b.1924   (div.)

Elizabeth Sarah Lavinia = Neil McCorquodale
b.1955

Cynthia Jane = Robert Fellowe
b.1957

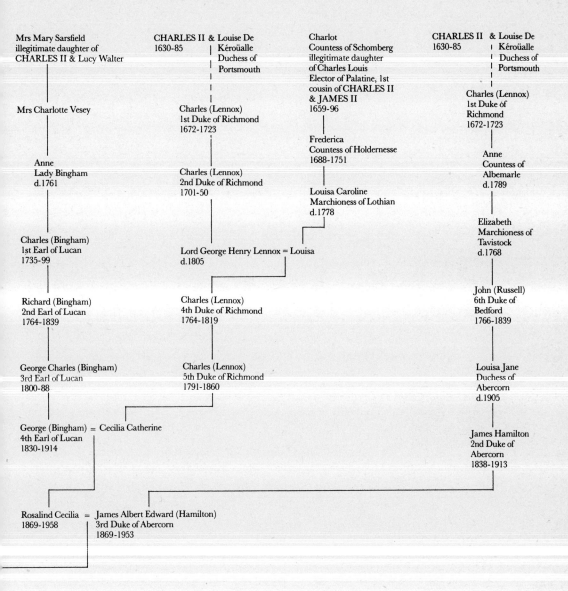

Mrs Mary Sarsfield
illegitimate daughter of
CHARLES II & Lucy Walter

Mrs Charlotte Vesey

Anne
Lady Bingham
d.1761

Charles (Bingham)
1st Earl of Lucan
1735-99

Richard (Bingham)
2nd Earl of Lucan
1764-1839

George Charles (Bingham)
3rd Earl of Lucan
1800-88

George (Bingham) = Cecilia Catherine
4th Earl of Lucan
1830-1914

CHARLES II & Louise De
1630-85   Kéroüalle
             Duchess of
             Portsmouth

Charles (Lennox)
1st Duke of Richmond
1672-1723

Charles (Lennox)
2nd Duke of Richmond
1701-50

Lord George Henry Lennox = Louisa
d.1805

Charles (Lennox)
4th Duke of Richmond
1764-1819

Charles (Lennox)
5th Duke of Richmond
1791-1860

Charlot
Countess of Schomberg
illegitimate daughter
of Charles Louis
Elector of Palatine, 1st
cousin of CHARLES II
& JAMES II
1659-96

Frederica
Countess of Holdernesse
1688-1751

Louisa Caroline
Marchioness of Lothian
d.1778

CHARLES II & Louise De
1630-85   Kéroüalle
             Duchess of
             Portsmouth

Charles (Lennox)
1st Duke of
Richmond
1672-1723

Anne
Countess of
Albemarle
d.1789

Elizabeth
Marchioness of
Tavistock
d.1768

John (Russell)
6th Duke of
Bedford
1766-1839

Louisa Jane
Duchess of
Abercorn
d.1905

James Hamilton
2nd Duke of
Abercorn
1838-1913

Rosalind Cecilia = James Albert Edward (Hamilton)
1869-1958   3rd Duke of Abercorn
                 1869-1953

Diana Frances
b. 1961

Charles Edward Maurice
Viscount Althorp
b.1964

Lady Diana Spencer belongs to that group of great historic families who hold earldoms, all earls being officially styled 'beloved Cousins' by the sovereign. Father to son, her direct forefathers have been earls since 1643, when Henry, third Lord Spencer was created Earl of Sunderland. Six of them have also been Knights of the Garter.

Towards the end of the Middle Ages, when wool was so important to England that the Lord Chancellor presided over the House of Lords while sitting (as he still does) on the Woolsack, the Spencers had made a great fortune from sheep. Under the Tudors they acquired Althorp, where the stately home now belonging to Lady Diana's father was built; and in 1603 Sir Robert Spencer was one of the first Peers of England to be created by the new Stuart king, James I, as first Baron Spencer. The third Earl fell in the Battle of Newbury at the age of twenty-three, a loyal Cavalier in the Civil War.

The Spencer family divided into two branches when Charles Spencer, third Earl of Sunderland, KG, married Lady Anne Churchill, daughter and co-heiress of the celebrated Duke of Marlborough, victor of Blenheim and one of the great strategists of all time, who was son of that staunch royalist, the original Sir Winston Churchill. The elder Spencer son's branch inherited the Churchill dukedom of Marlborough and Blenheim Palace, as well as the Spencer earldom of Sunderland, and took the surname of Spencer Churchill (its most distinguished member being the late Sir Winston Spencer Churchill). The younger branch, created Earls Spencer in 1765, inherited the old Spencer estates at Althorp. The third Earl Spencer, Chancellor of the Exchequer, declined the office of Prime Minister.

Lady Diana's mother, born the Hon. Frances Ruth Burke Roche, daughter of the fourth Lord Fermoy, is a quarter Irish, a quarter American and half Scottish. Her Roche ancestors, with their 'canting' Arms of three swimming roaches, were Norman-Irish, intermarried with such native Irish families as Hennessy. But the third Lord Fermoy married the daughter of the New York banker Frank Work, bringing in a descent from the Strong family of New England pioneer stock. In an article in the *Guardian* in March 1981, Stephen Cook wrote the following account of the 'black sheep' in Lady Diana's family:

> An examination of the American connection in the family of Prince Charles's bride-to-be reveals some intriguing goings-on in the nineteenth century and a person who could arguably be called a black sheep.
>
> This was Lady Diana Spencer's great-grandmother, Frances, daughter of the eccentric Mr Frank Work of New York, who wisely chose the career of stockbroker to the Vanderbilt family and amassed a large fortune.
>
> Mr Work strongly disapproved of the contemporary syndrome of American money marrying into European aristocracy, and threatened to disinherit any of his children who gave in to it. Frances immediately defied him by marrying James Boothby Burke Roche, heir to the second Baron Fermoy, a family of impeccable Irish blood but uncertain fortune.
>
> Eleven years later in 1891, Frances was back in New York, divorcing her aristocratic husband, and asking her father to relent and take her back with her three children.
>
> Mr Work did so, but made a will saying they would only inherit providing they changed their name back to Work, promised never to go to Europe for more than a holiday, and generally promised to be good Americans.
>
> Things appeared to go swimmingly until Mr Work discovered, four years before he died in 1911, that Frances was running around with Mr Auriel Botanyi, who was not only from Romania, but did work connected with horses. She married him and there was another row.
>
> After Mr Work died, a disappointed man, his grandson, Frances's eldest son Edmund Maurice, promptly broke the terms of the old man's will by climbing aboard the *Lusitania*, crossing to England, and standing in line for the Fermoy title, which he duly inherited in 1920. He was Lady Diana's grandfather.
>
> But his mother Frances stole the show again by sweeping over to England in 1931 for the marriage of her son to Ruth Gill, of Aberdeenshire.

Ruth, Lady Fermoy, widow of the fourth Lord Fermoy, who is Lady Diana's grandmother (and a close friend of Queen Elizabeth The Queen Mother) is a Gill of solid Aberdeenshire ancestry.

Lady Diana's father, the eighth Earl Spencer, on the other hand, belongs to the English high Whig aristocracy. Through him, the new Princess of Wales descends from many of the famous characters who made England's history: among them the second Earl Grey, the Prime Minister who passed the Great Reform Bill of 1832; the field-marshal fourth Earl of Lucan, who saved the Heavy Brigade when the Light Brigade charged into the valley of death in the

Crimea; the field-marshal first Marquess of Anglesey, who as Earl of Uxbridge lost his leg commanding the Cavalry at Waterloo; the fourth Duke of Richmond, who died of hydrophobia from a fox bite while Governor-General of Canada in 1819; and, in earlier centuries, from such figures as the great admiral first Earl Howe, the great soldiers Marlborough and Peterborough, Sir Richard Grenville of *The Revenge*, the first Duke of Somerset (Protector of England, beheaded during the minority of his nephew King Edward VI), the gallant Sidneys, Harry 'Hotspur' Lord Percy (the hero of Chevy Chase), and the great Simon de Montfort, Earl of Leicester, the founder of Parliament. Many of these descents she shares with Prince Charles: their nearest common ancestors were William Cavendish, third Duke of Devonshire, KG, who died in 1755, and his Duchess, who died in 1777.

But Lady Diana's most significant ancestors are, of course, those royal ones from whom Prince Charles does not himself descend. His Royal Highness descends from almost every sovereign of England and Scotland who left descendants, with the notable exception of Charles I, Charles II and James VII and II. Lady Diana, on the other hand, has no less than six direct descents from King Charles I, five of them through Charles II and one through James II's 'liaison' with Arabella Churchill, sister of the great Duke of Marlborough. These descents are, of course, all through 'natural children' of these two royal brothers, as Charles II had no lawful issue, and James II's lawful descendants are long extinct. This makes Lady Diana, therefore, one of the nearest living relations of Bonnie Prince Charlie: his first cousin, so many generations removed.

Lady Diana also brings to the Royal Family another royal descent they do not have: from King Henri Quatre of France, the dashing *vert galant* of the House of Bourbon, and his Queen, Marie de Medici, daughter of Francesco, Grand Duke of Tuscany (1574–87), son of the famous Grand Duke Cosimo de Medici – and sprung by a cousin marriage within the great Florentine houses from both Lorenzo the Magnificent and Giovanni *delle Bande Nera*. However, Queen Marie de Medici's mother was the Habsburg Archduchess Joanna, daughter of the Emperor Ferdinand I, from another of whose daughters Prince Charles descends. So both Lady Diana and Prince Charles share a descent through this emperor from innumerable historic sovereigns all over Christendom, such as Ferdinand and Isabella of Spain, who sent Columbus to the discovery of America – and whose daughter, Catherine of Aragon, was the third Princess of Wales before becoming Henry VIII's first Queen.

Lady Diana has yet another descent from King James I of England, through a natural daughter of Charles Lewis, Elector Palatine of the Rhine, son of the

'Winter Queen' of Bohemia. Thus, through her seven lines of descent from Mary Queen of Scots and the ill-fated Darnley, Lady Diana descends fourteen times over, albeit illegitimately, from King Henry VII and his Queen, the Plantaganet heiress. But she also has a fifteenth descent from them which is perfectly lawful. For, through the great peerage Houses of Abercorn, Bedford, Gordon, Aberdeen, Atholl, Derby and Cumberland, Lady Diana descends from the Princess Mary Tudor, Queen Dowager of France and Duchess of Brandon, sister of King Henry VIII. Through her grandmother, Lady Cynthia Eleanor Hamilton, she also descends lawfully from the first Lord Hamilton's wife, the Princess Mary Stewart, sister of James III, King of Scots, through whom the Hamiltons were long potential heirs presumptive to the Scottish throne.

Through both Mary Queen of Scots, and Charlotte de la Tremoille, Countess of Derby (grand-daughter of William the Silent, Prince of Orange, founder of the Dutch Republic, and great-grand-daughter of the celebrated Anne, duc de Montmorency, high constable of France), Lady Diana has links which carry her royal ancestry far back into the Ancient World. By way of the Dukes of Savoy and the Lusignan crusader kings of Cyprus and Jerusalem, Lady Diana descends many times over – like Prince Charles – from the Arsacid Great Kings of Parthia, whose dynasty was founded in 247 BC (before the first Chin 'universal emperor' of China) and who reigned over Persia and Babylonia more than two thousand years ago.

APPENDIX C

The Ancestral Link between Prince Charles and Lady Diana

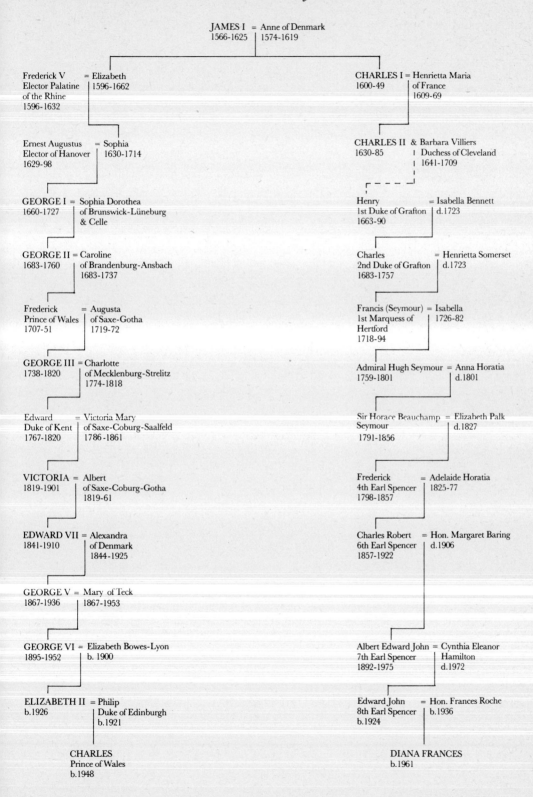

JAMES I = Anne of Denmark
1566-1625 | 1574-1619

Frederick V = Elizabeth
Elector Palatine | 1596-1662
of the Rhine
1596-1632

CHARLES I = Henrietta Maria
1600-49 | of France
1609-69

Ernest Augustus = Sophia
Elector of Hanover | 1630-1714
1629-98

CHARLES II & Barbara Villiers
1630-85 | Duchess of Cleveland
1641-1709

GEORGE I = Sophia Dorothea
1660-1727 | of Brunswick-Lüneburg
& Celle

Henry = Isabella Bennett
1st Duke of Grafton | d.1723
1663-90

GEORGE II = Caroline
1683-1760 | of Brandenburg-Ansbach
1683-1737

Charles = Henrietta Somerset
2nd Duke of Grafton | d.1723
1683-1757

Frederick = Augusta
Prince of Wales | of Saxe-Gotha
1707-51 | 1719-72

Francis (Seymour) = Isabella
1st Marquess of | 1726-82
Hertford
1718-94

GEORGE III = Charlotte
1738-1820 | of Mecklenburg-Strelitz
1774-1818

Admiral Hugh Seymour = Anna Horatia
1759-1801 | d.1801

Edward = Victoria Mary
Duke of Kent | of Saxe-Coburg-Saalfeld
1767-1820 | 1786-1861

Sir Horace Beauchamp = Elizabeth Palk
Seymour | d.1827
1791-1856

VICTORIA = Albert
1819-1901 | of Saxe-Coburg-Gotha
1819-61

Frederick = Adelaide Horatia
4th Earl Spencer | 1825-77
1798-1857

EDWARD VII = Alexandra
1841-1910 | of Denmark
1844-1925

Charles Robert = Hon. Margaret Baring
6th Earl Spencer | d.1906
1857-1922

GEORGE V = Mary of Teck
1867-1936 | 1867-1953

GEORGE VI = Elizabeth Bowes-Lyon
1895-1952 | b. 1900

Albert Edward John = Cynthia Eleanor
7th Earl Spencer | Hamilton
1892-1975 | d.1972

ELIZABETH II = Philip
b.1926 | Duke of Edinburgh
b.1921

Edward John = Hon. Frances Roche
8th Earl Spencer | b.1936
b.1924

CHARLES
Prince of Wales
b.1948

DIANA FRANCES
b.1961

APPENDIX D

The Previous English Princes and Princesses of Wales

(The year of investiture is shown in brackets)

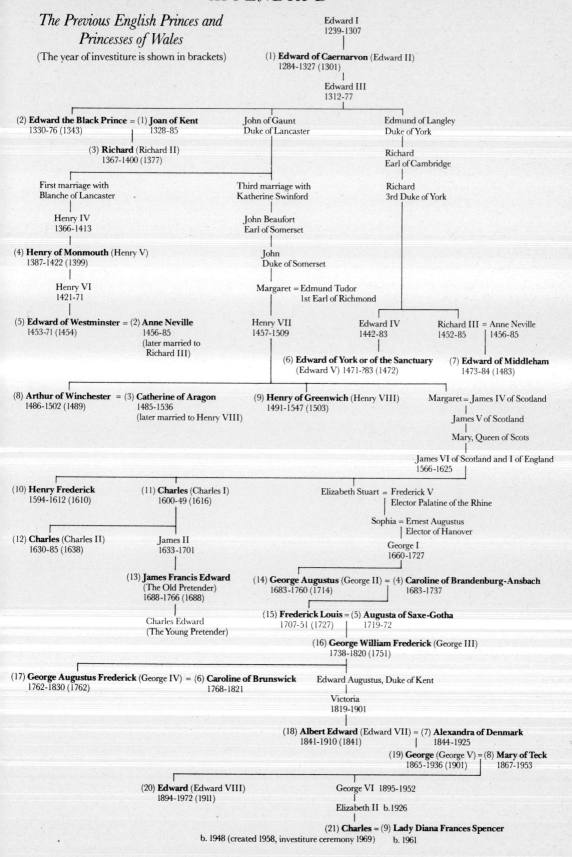

Edward I
1239-1307

(1) **Edward of Caernarvon** (Edward II)
1284-1327 (1301)

Edward III
1312-77

(2) **Edward the Black Prince** = (1) **Joan of Kent**
1330-76 (1343)   1328-85

John of Gaunt
Duke of Lancaster

Edmund of Langley
Duke of York

(3) **Richard** (Richard II)
1367-1400 (1377)

Richard
Earl of Cambridge

First marriage with
Blanche of Lancaster

Third marriage with
Katherine Swinford

Richard
3rd Duke of York

Henry IV
1366-1413

John Beaufort
Earl of Somerset

(4) **Henry of Monmouth** (Henry V)
1387-1422 (1399)

John
Duke of Somerset

Henry VI
1421-71

Margaret = Edmund Tudor
1st Earl of Richmond

(5) **Edward of Westminster** = (2) **Anne Neville**
1453-71 (1454)   1456-85
(later married to
Richard III)

Henry VII
1457-1509

Edward IV
1442-83

Richard III = Anne Neville
1452-85   1456-85

(6) **Edward of York or of the Sanctuary**
(Edward V) 1471-?83 (1472)

(7) **Edward of Middleham**
1473-84 (1483)

(8) **Arthur of Winchester** = (3) **Catherine of Aragon**
1486-1502 (1489)   1485-1536
(later married to Henry VIII)

(9) **Henry of Greenwich** (Henry VIII)
1491-1547 (1503)

Margaret = James IV of Scotland

James V of Scotland

Mary, Queen of Scots

James VI of Scotland and I of England
1566-1625

(10) **Henry Frederick**
1594-1612 (1610)

(11) **Charles** (Charles I)
1600-49 (1616)

Elizabeth Stuart = Frederick V
Elector Palatine of the Rhine

Sophia = Ernest Augustus
Elector of Hanover

(12) **Charles** (Charles II)
1630-85 (1638)

James II
1633-1701

George I
1660-1727

(13) **James Francis Edward**
(The Old Pretender)
1688-1766 (1688)

(14) **George Augustus** (George II) = (4) **Caroline of Brandenburg-Ansbach**
1683-1760 (1714)   1683-1737

Charles Edward
(The Young Pretender)

(15) **Frederick Louis** = (5) **Augusta of Saxe-Gotha**
1707-51 (1727)   1719-72

(16) **George William Frederick** (George III)
1738-1820 (1751)

(17) **George Augustus Frederick** (George IV) = (6) **Caroline of Brunswick**
1762-1830 (1762)   1768-1821

Edward Augustus, Duke of Kent

Victoria
1819-1901

(18) **Albert Edward** (Edward VII) = (7) **Alexandra of Denmark**
1841-1910 (1841)   1844-1925

(19) **George** (George V) = (8) **Mary of Teck**
1865-1936 (1901)   1867-1953

(20) **Edward** (Edward VIII)
1894-1972 (1911)

George VI 1895-1952

Elizabeth II b.1926

(21) **Charles** = (9) **Lady Diana Frances Spencer**
b. 1948 (created 1958, investiture ceremony 1969)   b. 1961

Rhodri the Great	844-78
Anarawd, son of Rhodri	878-916
Hywel Dda, the Good	916-50
Iago ab Idwal (or Ieuaf)	950-79
Hywel ab Ieuaf, the Bad	979-85
Cadwallon, brother of Hywel	985-86
Maredudd ab Owain ap Hywel Dda	986-99
Cynan ap Hywel ab Ieuaf	999-1008
Llewelyn ap Sitsyhlt	1018-23
Iago ab Idwal ap Meurig	1023-39
Gruffydd ap Llewelyn ap Seisyll	1039-63
Bleddyn ap Cynfyn	1063-75
Trahaern ap Caradog	1075-81
Gruffydd ap Cynan ab Iago	1081-1137
Owain Gwynedd	1137-70
Dafydd ab Owain Gwynedd	1170-94
Llewelyn Fawr, the Great	1194-1240
Dafydd ap Llewelyn	1240-46
Llewelyn ap Gruffydd ap Llewelyn	1246-82

		Date created
Edward of Caernarvon (Edward II), son of Edward I	1284–1327	1301
Edward the Black Prince, eldest son of Edward III	1330–76	1343
Richard (Richard II), younger son of the Black Prince	1367–1400	1377
Henry of Monmouth (Henry V), eldest son of Henry IV	1387–1422	1399
Edward of Westminster, only son of Henry VI	1453–71	1454
Edward of York (Edward V), eldest son of Edward IV	1470–83	1472
Edward of Middleham, son of Richard III	1473–84	1483
Arthur of Winchester, eldest son of Henry VII	1486–1502	1489
Henry of Greenwich (Henry VIII), second son of Henry VII	1491–1547	1503
Henry Frederick, eldest son of James I and VI	1594–1612	1610
Charles (Charles I), second son of James I and VI	1600–49	1616
Charles (Charles II), second son of Charles I	1630–85	1638
James, the old Pretender, son of James II	1688–1766	1688
George Augustus (George II), son of George I	1683–1760	1714
Frederick Louis, eldest son of George II	1707–51	1727
George William Frederick (George III), son of Frederick Louis	1738–1820	1751
George Augustus Frederick (George IV), son of George III	1762–1830	1762
Albert Edward (Edward VII), eldest son of Queen Victoria	1841–1910	1841
George (George V), second son of Edward VII	1865–1936	1901
Edward (Edward VIII, later Duke of Windsor), eldest son of George V	1894–1972	1910
Charles Philip Arthur George, eldest son of Elizabeth II	1948–	1958

		Married
Joan of Kent, wife of Edward the Black Prince	1328–85	1361
Anne Neville, wife of Edward of Westminster; widowed in 1471, she later married Richard III	1456–85	1470
Catherine of Aragon, wife of Arthur of Winchester; widowed in 1502, she later married Henry VIII	1485–1536	1501
Caroline of Brandenburg-Ansbach, wife of George Augustus (George II)	1683–1737	1706
Augusta of Saxe-Gotha, wife of Frederick Louis	1719–72	1736
Caroline of Brunswick, wife of George Augustus Frederick (George IV)	1768–1821	1795
Alexandra of Denmark, wife of Albert Edward (Edward VII)	1844–1925	1863
Mary of Teck, wife of George (George V)	1867–1953	1893
Lady Diana Spencer, wife of Charles Philip Arthur George	1961–	1981

BIBLIOGRAPHY

This is an updated version of the bibliography of *Charles, Prince of Wales*, and refers the reader both to books consulted and to books which would answer the needs of those seeking more detailed information in specialist areas.

ARNOLD-BROWN, ADAM, *Unfolding Character: The Impact of Gordonstoun*, Routledge & Kegan Paul, 1962.

ASHDOWN, DULCIE M., *Princesses of Wales*, John Murray, 1979.

BAGEHOT, WALTER, *The English Constitution*, Chapman & Hall, 1867; Longmans, Green, 1915.

BEATON, CECIL WALTER HARDY, *Photobiography*, Odhams Press, 1951.

BEAVERBROOK, WILLIAM MAXWELL AITKEN, Baron, *The Abdication of King Edward VIII* (edited by A. J. P. Taylor), Hamish Hamilton, 1966.

BIRCH, NEVILLE HAMILTON and ALAN BRAMSON, *Captains & Kings*, Pitman, 1972.

BOOTHROYD, JOHN BASIL, *Philip: An Informal Biography*, Longman, 1971.

BRERETON, HENRY LLOYD, *Gordonstoun: Ancient Estate and Modern School*, W. & R. Chambers, 1968.

BROOKE, JOHN, *King George III*, with a foreword by HRH the Prince of Wales, Constable, 1972.

CATHCART, HELEN, *Prince Charles: The Biography*, W. H. Allen, 1976.

CHANNON, SIR HENRY, '*Chips': The Diaries of Sir Henry Channon* (edited by Robert Rhodes James), Weidenfeld & Nicolson, 1967.

CHARLES, PRINCE OF WALES, 'Legend and Reality', a review of *Queen Victoria Was Amused* by Alan Hardy, *Books and Bookmen*, November 1976.

CHARLES, PRINCE OF WALES, Review (unheadlined) of *Twice Brightly*, a novel by Harry Secombe, *Punch*, 6 November 1974.

COOLICAN, DON and LEMOINE, SERGE, *Charles: Royal Adventurer*, Pelham Books, 1978.

COUNIHAN, DANIEL, *Royal Progress*, Cassell, 1977.

CRAWFORD, MARION, *The Little Princess*, Cassell, 1950.

DONALDSON, FRANCES LONSDALE, LADY, *Edward VIII*, Weidenfeld & Nicolson, 1974.

DORAN, JOHN, *The Book of the Princes of Wales, Heirs to the Crown of England*, R. Bentley, 1860.

DUNCAN, ANDREW, *The Reality of Monarch*, Heinemann, 1970.

EDGAR, DONALD, *The Queen's Children*, Arthur Barker, 1978.

EDWARD VIII, King of Great Britain, *A Family Album* by the Duke of Windsor, Cassell, 1960.

EDWARD VIII, King of Great Britain, *A King's Story: The Memoirs of H.R.H. the Duke of Windsor*, Cassell, 1951.

FISHER, GRAHAM and HEATHER, *Charles: The Man and the Prince*, Hale, 1977.

GORE, JOHN, *King George V, A Personal Memoir*, John Murray, 1941.

HIBBERT, CHRISTOPHER, *The Court of St James's*, Weidenfeld & Nicolson, 1979.

HOLDEN, ANTHONY, *Charles, Prince of Wales*, Weidenfeld & Nicolson, 1979.

INGLIS, BRIAN, *Abdication*, Hodder & Stoughton, 1966.

IWI, EDWARD, 'Mountbatten-Windsor', *The Law Journal*, 18 March 1960.

JUDD, DENIS, *Prince Philip, Duke of Edinburgh*, Michael Joseph, 1980.

LACEY, ROBERT, *Majesty: Elizabeth II and the House of Windsor*, Hutchinson, 1977.

LAIRD, DOROTHY, *How the Queen Reigns: An Authentic Study of the Queen's Personality and Life Work*, Hodder & Stoughton, 1959.

LANE, PETER, *Our Future King*, Arthur Barker, 1978.

LIVERSIDGE, DOUGLAS, *Prince Charles: Monarch in the Making*, Arthur Barker, 1975.

MAGNUS, SIR PHILIP, *King Edward VII*, John Murray, 1964.

MARPLES, MORRIS, *Princes in the Making: A Study of Royal Education*, Faber and Faber, 1965.

MARTIN, KINGSLEY, *The Crown and the Establishment*, Hutchinson, 1962.

MASTERS, BRIAN, *Dreams about H.M. The Queen and Other Members of the Royal Family*; illustrated by Michael Ffolkes, Blond and Briggs, 1972.

MILLIGAN, TERENCE ALAN, *More Goon Show Scripts*, written and selected by Spike Milligan; with drawings by Peter Sellers, Harry Secombe, Spike Milligan, Woburn Press, 1973.

MORRAH, DERMOT, *To Be A King*, Hutchinson, 1968.

NICOLSON, HON. HAROLD GEORGE, *King George the Fifth: His Life and Reign*, Constable, 1952.

PAGET, GERALD, *The Lineage and Ancestry of HRH Prince Charles, Prince of Wales*, 2 vols, Skilton, 1977.

PALMER, ALAN, *Princes of Wales*, Weidenfeld & Nicolson, 1979.

PEACOCK, IRENE CYNTHIA, Lady, *The Queen and Her Children: An Authoritative Account*, Hutchinson, 1961.

PEEL, EDWARD, *Cheam School from 1645*, Thornhill Press, 1974.

PINE, LESLIE GILBERT, *Princes of Wales*, Herbert Jenkins, 1959.

POPE-HENNESSY, JAMES, *Queen Mary, 1867–1953*, G. Allen & Unwin, 1959.

RÖHRS, HERMANN, *Kurt Hahn*; from the German edition. English edn, with additional material; edited by H. Röhrs and H. Tunstall-Behrens; preface by the Duke of Edinburgh; Routledge & Kegan Paul, 1970.

BIBLIOGRAPHY

ST JOHN-STEVAS, NORMAN, *Walter Bagehot*, published for the British Council and the National Book League by Longmans, Green, 1963.

SIDNEY, THOMAS, *Heirs Apparent*, Allan Wingate, 1957.

SKIDELSKY, ROBERT JACOB ALEXANDER, *Hahn of Gordonstoun*, Penguin, 1969.

STEWART, WILLIAM ALEXANDER CAMPBELL, *The Thirties and Gordonstoun*, Macmillan, 1968.

TALBOT, GODFREY, *The Country Life Book of Queen Elizabeth the Queen Mother*, Country Life Books, 1978.

WAKEFORD, GEOFFREY, *The Heir Apparent: An Authentic Study of the Life and Training of H.R.H. Charles Prince of Wales*, Hale, 1967.

WARREN, ALLEN, *Nobs and Nosh*, Leslie Frewin, 1974.

WARWICK, CHRISTOPHER, *Two Centuries of Royal Weddings*, Arthur Barker, 1980.

WHITAKER, JAMES, *Prince Charles*, City Magazines Ltd, 1978.

ZIEGLER, PHILIP, *Crown and People*, Collins, 1978.

INDEX

Abercorn, Dowager Duchess of, 43
Abercorn, Dukes of, 30
Abercorn, 3rd Duke of, 39
Acklom, Esther, 38
Act of Settlement (1701), 48, 97
Adams, John, 39
Adeane, Edward, 46, 122
Adeane, Sir Michael, 116
Airlie, Lady, 103, 105
Die Aktuelle, 61
Albert, Prince Consort, 38, 41, 78, 85-6, 88-9, 108
Albert Victor, Prince (Prince Eddy), 40, 99, 100
Alexander II, Tsar, 87
Alexandra, Princess, 23, 52, 79
Alexandra, Queen, consort of Edward VII, 18, 19, 41, 43, 66, 86-90, 99, 100, 108
Alexandrine, Princess of Prussia, 86
Alice, Princess, 79
Allen, Gertrude, 31
Allibar, 41
Althorp, Charles, Viscount, 30, 32
Althorp, Northamptonshire, 32, 36-8, 60, 80
Amalgamated Society of Woodworkers, Camden Town First Branch, 114
Andrew, Prince, 29, 31, 34, 52, 57-8, 71, 84, 111
Anna, Princess of Hesse, 86
Anne, Princess, 41, 47, 57, 63, 70, 74-6, 81-2, 84, 109-12, 120, 123

Anne, Queen of England, 37, 41, 93, 94
Anne Catherine, Queen of Denmark, 36
Ansbach, Margrave of, 93-4
Ardencaple, 31
Argyllshire, 31
Armstrong-Jones, Lady Sarah, 110
Army Catering Corps, 110
Arthur, Prince of Wales, 93, 108
Ascot, 60, 61
Ashcombe, Lord, 70
Ashdown, Dulcie M., 112
Astor, Lord, 68
Astor, Louise, 68
Attlee, Clement, 75
Augusta, Princess of Meiningen, 86
Augusta, Princess of Wales, 95-7, 112
Australia, 23, 30, 51, 70, 82-4, 90

Bagehot, Walter, 117, 118, 119
Baker, Maureen, 109
Baldwin, Stanley, 54, 119
Balmoral, 48, 54, 60-1, 78, 125
Balniel, Lord, 67
Bayer (UK), 33
BBC, 69, 107, 108
Beatrix, Queen of the Netherlands, 116
Beaufort, Duke of, 77
Beaufort Hunt, 77
Beaverbrook, Lord, 105
Bedford, Dukes of, 30
Bedford, 4th Duke of, 35

Bentinck, Bill (later Duke of Portland), 33
Berkshire Downs, 64
Berlioz, Hector, 55
Bessborough, Lady Henrietta, 37
Bill of Rights (1689), 48
Bingham family, 30
Bingham, Lady Lavinia, 38
Birch, Henry, 89
Birkhall, 61
Birmingham Mint, 24
Black and Edgington, 24
Blake, Lord, 117
Boothby, Brooke, 68
Boothroyd, Basil, 102-3
Brabourne, Lady, 42
Brabourne, Lord, 42
Bristol, Countess of, 37
Britannia, HMS, 111
British Tourist Authority, 24
Broadlands, Hampshire, 106
Bronington, HMS, 25
Brooks-Baker, Harold, 39
Buckingham Palace, 23, 25, 26, 46, 50, 75, 81, 105, 116
Bute, John Stuart, Earl of, 97
Butler, Lord, 51, 76
Buxton family, 67
Buxton, Aubrey, 67

Cabarrus, Count Pierre de, 67
Caernarvon, 51, 73
Callaghan, James, 47, 53, 80
Cambridge, Duchess of, 87
Cambridge University, 51, 67

[155]